DATE DUE

JA 18 '92	NO 2 '96	DE 9 '04	
MY 22 '92	DE 17 '98		
JY 31 '92	MY 27 '98		
AG 27 '92			
NO 30 '92	DE 18 '98		
JA	MY 24 '99		
MY 21 '93	AP 14 '00		
NO			
JA 14 '94	AP 24 '00		
JE 18 '94	DE 2 '00		
MY 26 '95	MY 13 '02		
	DE 5 '02		
AP 26 '96	DE 24 '02		
JY 25 '96			
DE 17 '97	FE 13 '03		

Demco, Inc. 38-293

SUICIDE

GENERAL EDITORS

Dale C. Garell, M.D.
Medical Director, California Children Services, Department of Health
    Services, County of Los Angeles
Associate Dean for Curriculum; Clinical Professor, Department of Pediatrics &
    Family Medicine, University of Southern California School of Medicine
Former President, Society for Adolescent Medicine

Solomon H. Snyder, M.D.
Distinguished Service Professor of Neuroscience, Pharmacology, and
    Psychiatry, Johns Hopkins University School of Medicine
Former President, Society for Neuroscience
Albert Lasker Award in Medical Research, 1978

CONSULTING EDITORS

Robert W. Blum, M.D., Ph.D.
Associate Professor, School of Public Health and Department of
    Pediatrics
Director, Adolescent Health Program, University of Minnesota
    Consultant, World Health Organization

Charles E. Irwin, Jr., M.D.
Associate Professor of Pediatrics; Director, Division of Adolescent
    Medicine, University of California, San Francisco

Lloyd J. Kolbe, Ph.D.
Chief, Office of School Health & Special Projects, Center for Health
    Promotion & Education, Centers for Disease Control
President, American School Health Association

Jordan J. Popkin
Director, Division of Federal Employee Occupational Health, U.S. Public
    Health Service Region I

Joseph L. Rauh, M.D.
Professor of Pediatrics and Medicine, Adolescent Medicine, Children's
    Hospital Medical Center, Cincinnati
Former President, Society for Adolescent Medicine

THE ENCYCLOPEDIA OF
H E A L T H

PSYCHOLOGICAL DISORDERS
AND THEIR TREATMENT

Solomon H. Snyder, M.D. · General Editor

SUICIDE

Laura Dolce

Introduction by C. Everett Koop, M.D., Sc.D.

former Surgeon General, U. S. Public Health Service

CHELSEA HOUSE PUBLISHERS

New York · Philadelphia

l is to provide general information in
ychology, and related medical issues.
to take the place of the professional
e professional.

The personal accounts included in *Suicide* are true, but names, and places have been
changed to protect those involved.

ON THE COVER: *Melancholia* (1891–92) by Edvard Munch

Chelsea House Publishers

EDITOR-IN-CHIEF   Remmel Nunn
MANAGING EDITOR   Karyn Gullen Browne
COPY CHIEF   Juliann Barbato
PICTURE EDITOR   Adrian G. Allen
ART DIRECTOR   Maria Epes
DEPUTY COPY CHIEF   Mark Rifkin
ASSISTANT ART DIRECTOR   Noreen Romano
MANUFACTURING MANAGER   Gerald Levine
SYSTEMS MANAGER   Lindsey Ottman
PRODUCTION MANAGER   Joseph Romano
PRODUCTION COORDINATOR   Marie Claire Cebrián

The Encyclopedia of Health

SENIOR EDITOR   Brian Feinberg

Staff for SUICIDE

ASSOCIATE EDITOR   LaVonne Carlson-Finnerty
COPY EDITOR   Laurie Kahn
EDITORIAL ASSISTANTS   Christopher Duffy, Tamar Levovitz
PICTURE RESEARCHER   Georganne Backman Garfinkel
DESIGNER   Robert Yaffe

Library of Congress Cataloging-in-Publication Data

Dolce, Laura.
   I. Suicide/by Laura Dolce; introduction by C. Everett Koop.
   p.   cm.—(The Encyclopedia of Health. Psychological disorders and their treatment)
   Includes bibliography and index.
   Summary: Discusses the social, psychological, medical, and historical facets of
suicide, describing warning signs, risk factors, prevention, and other aspects.
      ISBN 0-7910-0053-2
      0-7910-0517-8 (pbk.)
   1. Suicide—Juvenile literature. [1. Suicide.] I. Title. II. Series.   91-9868
HV6545.L73 1991   CIP
362.28—dc20   AC

CONTENTS

THE ENCYCLOPEDIA OF
H E A L T H

THE HEALTHY BODY

The Circulatory System
Dental Health
The Digestive System
The Endocrine System
Exercise
Genetics & Heredity
The Human Body: An Overview
Hygiene
The Immune System
Memory & Learning
The Musculoskeletal System
The Nervous System
Nutrition
The Reproductive System
The Respiratory System
The Senses
Sleep
Speech & Hearing
Sports Medicine
Vision
Vitamins & Minerals

THE LIFE CYCLE

Adolescence
Adulthood
Aging
Childhood
Death & Dying
The Family
Friendship & Love
Pregnancy & Birth

MEDICAL ISSUES

Careers in Health Care
Environmental Health
Folk Medicine
Health Care Delivery
Holistic Medicine
Medical Ethics
Medical Fakes & Frauds
Medical Technology
Medicine & the Law
Occupational Health
Public Health

PSYCHOLOGICAL DISORDERS AND THEIR TREATMENT

Anxiety & Phobias
Child Abuse
Compulsive Behavior
Delinquency & Criminal Behavior
Depression
Diagnosing & Treating Mental Illness
Eating Habits & Disorders
Learning Disabilities
Mental Retardation
Personality Disorders
Schizophrenia
Stress Management
Suicide

MEDICAL DISORDERS AND THEIR TREATMENT

AIDS
Allergies
Alzheimer's Disease
Arthritis
Birth Defects
Cancer
The Common Cold
Diabetes
Emergency Medicine
Gynecological Disorders
Headaches
The Hospital
Kidney Disorders
Medical Diagnosis
The Mind-Body Connection
Mononucleosis and Other Infectious Diseases
Nuclear Medicine
Organ Transplants
Pain
Physical Handicaps
Poisons & Toxins
Prescription & OTC Drugs
Sexually Transmitted Diseases
Skin Disorders
Stroke & Heart Disease
Substance Abuse
Tropical Medicine

PREVENTION AND EDUCATION: THE KEYS TO GOOD HEALTH

C. Everett Koop, M.D., Sc.D.
former Surgeon General,
U.S. Public Health Service

The issue of health education has received particular attention in recent years because of the presence of AIDS in the news. But our response to this particular tragedy points up a number of broader issues that doctors, public health officials, educators, and the public face. In particular, it points up the necessity for sound health education for citizens of all ages.

Over the past 25 years this country has been able to bring about dramatic declines in the death rates for heart disease, stroke, accidents, and for people under the age of 45, cancer. Today, Americans generally eat better and take better care of themselves than ever before. Thus, with the help of modern science and technology, they have a better chance of surviving serious—even catastrophic—illnesses. That's the good news.

But, like every phonograph record, there's a flip side, and one with special significance for young adults. According to a report issued in 1979 by Dr. Julius Richmond, my predecessor as Surgeon General, Americans aged 15 to 24 had a higher death rate in 1979 than they did 20 years earlier. The causes: violent death and injury, alcohol and drug abuse, unwanted pregnancies, and sexually transmitted diseases. Adolescents are particularly vulnerable because they are beginning to explore their own sexuality and perhaps to experiment with drugs. The need for educating young people is critical, and the price of neglect is high.

Yet even for the population as a whole, our health is still far from what it could be. Why? A 1974 Canadian government report attributed all death and disease to four broad elements: inadequacies in the health care system, behavioral factors or unhealthy life-styles, environmental hazards, and human biological factors.

To be sure, there are diseases that are still beyond the control of even our advanced medical knowledge and techniques. And despite yearnings that are as old as the human race itself, there is no "fountain of youth" to ward off aging and death. Still, there is a solution to many of the problems that undermine sound health. In a word, that solution is prevention. Prevention, which includes health promotion and education, saves lives, improves the quality of life, and in the long run, saves money.

In the United States, organized public health activities and preventive medicine have a long history. Important milestones in this country or foreign breakthroughs adopted in the United States include the improvement of sanitary procedures and the development of pasteurized milk in the late 19th century and the introduction in the mid-20th century of effective vaccines against polio, measles, German measles, mumps, and other once-rampant diseases. Internationally, organized public health efforts began on a wide-scale basis with the International Sanitary Conference of 1851, to which 12 nations sent representatives. The World Health Organization, founded in 1948, continues these efforts under the aegis of the United Nations, with particular emphasis on combating communicable diseases and the training of health care workers.

Despite these accomplishments, much remains to be done in the field of prevention. For too long, we have had a medical care system that is science- and technology-based, focused, essentially, on illness and mortality. It is now patently obvious that both the social and the economic costs of such a system are becoming insupportable.

Implementing prevention—and its corollaries, health education and promotion—is the job of several groups of people.

First, the medical and scientific professions need to continue basic scientific research, and here we are making considerable progress. But increased concern with prevention will also have a decided impact on how primary care doctors practice medicine. With a shift to health-based rather than morbidity-based medicine, the role of the "new physician" will include a healthy dose of patient education.

Second, practitioners of the social and behavioral sciences—psychologists, economists, city planners—along with lawyers, business leaders, and government officials—must solve the practical and ethical dilemmas confronting us: poverty, crime, civil rights, literacy, education, employment, housing, sanitation, environmental protection, health care delivery systems, and so forth. All of these issues affect public health.

Third is the public at large. We'll consider that very important group in a moment.

Fourth, and the linchpin in this effort, is the public health profession—doctors, epidemiologists, teachers—who must harness the professional expertise of the first two groups and the common sense and cooperation of the third, the public. They must define the problems statistically and qualitatively and then help us set priorities for finding the solutions.

To a very large extent, improving those statistics is the responsibility of every individual. So let's consider more specifically what the role of the individual should be and why health education is so important to that role. First, and most obvious, individuals can protect themselves from illness and injury and thus minimize their need for professional medical care. They can eat nutritious food; get adequate exercise; avoid tobacco, alcohol, and drugs; and take prudent steps to avoid accidents. The proverbial "apple a day keeps the doctor away" is not so far from the truth, after all.

Second, individuals should actively participate in their own medical care. They should schedule regular medical and dental checkups. Should they develop an illness or injury, they should know when to treat themselves and when to seek professional help. To gain the maximum benefit from any medical treatment that they do require, individuals must become partners in that treatment. For instance, they should understand the effects and side effects of medications. I counsel young physicians that there is no such thing as too much information when talking with patients. But the corollary is the patient must know enough about the nuts and bolts of the healing process to understand what the doctor is telling him or her. That is at least partially the patient's responsibility.

Education is equally necessary for us to understand the ethical and public policy issues in health care today. Sometimes individuals will encounter these issues in making decisions about their own treatment or that of family members. Other citizens may encounter them as jurors in medical malpractice cases. But we all become involved, indirectly, when we elect our public officials, from school board members to the president. Should surrogate parenting be legal? To what extent is drug testing desirable, legal, or necessary? Should there be public funding for family planning, hospitals, various types of medical research, and other medical care for the indigent? How should we allocate scant technological resources, such as kidney dialysis and organ transplants? What is the proper role of government in protecting the rights of patients?

What are the broad goals of public health in the United States today? In 1980, the Public Health Service issued a report aptly entitled *Promoting Health—Preventing Disease: Objectives for the Nation.* This report expressed its goals in terms of mortality and in terms of intermediate goals in education and health improvement. It identified 15 major concerns: controlling high blood pressure; improving family planning; improving pregnancy care and infant health; increasing the rate of immunization; controlling sexually transmitted diseases; controlling the presence of toxic agents and radiation in the environment; improving occupational safety and health; preventing accidents; promoting water fluoridation and dental health; controlling infectious diseases; decreasing smoking; decreasing alcohol and drug abuse; improving nutrition; promoting physical fitness and exercise; and controlling stress and violent behavior.

For healthy adolescents and young adults (ages 15 to 24), the specific goal was a 20% reduction in deaths, with a special focus on motor vehicle injuries and alcohol and drug abuse. For adults (ages 25 to 64), the aim was 25% fewer deaths, with a concentration on heart attacks, strokes, and cancers.

Smoking is perhaps the best example of how individual behavior can have a direct impact on health. Today, cigarette smoking is recognized as the single most important preventable cause of death in our society. It is responsible for more cancers and more cancer deaths than any other known agent; is a prime risk factor for heart and blood vessel disease, chronic bronchitis, and emphysema; and is a frequent cause of complications in pregnancies and of babies born prematurely, underweight, or with potentially fatal respiratory and cardiovascular problems.

Since the release of the Surgeon General's first report on smoking in 1964, the proportion of adult smokers has declined substantially, from 43% in 1965 to 30.5% in 1985. Since 1965, 37 million people have quit smoking. Although there is still much work to be done if we are to become a "smoke-free society," it is heartening to note that public health and public education efforts—such as warnings on cigarette packages and bans on broadcast advertising—have already had significant effects.

In 1835, Alexis de Tocqueville, a French visitor to America, wrote, "In America the passion for physical well-being is general." Today, as then, health and fitness are front-page items. But with the greater scientific and technological resources now available to us, we are in a far stronger position to make good health care available to everyone. And with the greater technological threats to us as we approach the 21st century, the need to do so is more urgent than ever before. Comprehensive information about basic biology, preventive medicine, medical and surgical treatments, and related ethical and public policy issues can help you arm yourself with the knowledge you need to be healthy throughout your life.

FOREWORD

Solomon H. Snyder, M.D.

Mental disorders represent the number one health problem for the United States and probably for the entire human population. Some studies estimate that approximately one-third of all Americans suffer from some sort of emotional disturbance. Depression of varying severity will affect as many as 20 percent of all of us at one time or another in our lives. Severe anxiety is even more common.

Adolescence is a time of particular susceptibility to emotional problems. Teenagers are undergoing significant changes in their brain as well as their physical structure. The hormones that alter the organs of reproduction during puberty also influence the way we think and feel. At a purely psychological level, adolescents must cope with major upheavals in their lives. After years of not noticing the opposite sex, they find themselves romantically attracted but must painfully learn the skills of social interchange both for superficial, flirtatious relationships and for genuine intimacy. Teenagers must develop new ways of relating to their parents. Adolescents strive for independence. Yet, our society is structured in such a way that teenagers must remain dependent on their parents for many more years. During adolescence, young men and women examine their own intellectual bents and begin to plan the type of higher education and vocation they believe they will find most fulfilling.

Because of these challenges, teenagers are more emotionally volatile than adults. Passages from extreme exuberance to dejection are common. The emotional distress of completely normal adolescence can be so severe that the same disability in an adult would be labeled as major mental illness. Although most teenagers somehow muddle through and emerge unscathed, a number of problems are more frequent among adolescents than among adults. Many psychological aberrations reflect severe disturbances, although these are sometimes not regarded as "psychiatric." Eating disorders, to which young adults are especially vulnerable, are an example. An extremely large number of teenagers diet to great excess even though they are not overweight. Many of them suffer from a specific disturbance referred to as anorexia nervosa, a form of self-starvation that is just as real a disorder as diabetes. the same is true for those who eat compulsively and then sometimes force themselves to vomit. They may be afflicted with bulimia.

Depression is also surprisingly frequent among adolescents, although its symptoms may be less obvious in young people than they are in adults. And, because suicide occurs most frequently in those suffering from depression, we must be on the lookout for subtle hints of despondency in those close to us. This is especially urgent because teenage suicide is a rapidly worsening national problem.

The volumes on Psychological Disorders and Their Treatment in the Encyclopedia Of Health cover the major areas of mental illness, from mild to severe. They also emphasize the means available for getting help. Anxiety and Phobias, Depression, and Schizophrenia deal specifically with these forms of mental disturbance. Child Abuse and Delinquency and Criminal Behavior explore abnormalities of behavior that may stem from environmental and social influences as much as from biological or psychological illness. Personality Disorders and Compulsive Behavior explain how people develop disturbances of their overall personality. Learning Disabilities investigates disturbances of the mind that may reflect neurological derangements as much as psychological abnormalities. Mental Retardation explains the various causes of this many-sided handicap, including the genetic component, complications during pregnancy, and traumas during birth. Suicide discusses the epidemiology of this tragic phenomenon and outlines the assistance available to those who are at risk. Stress Management locates the source of stress in contemporary society and considers formal strategies for coping with it. Finally, Diagnosing and Treating Mental Illness explains to the reader how professionals sift through various signs and symptoms to define the exact nature of the various mental disorders and fully describes the most effective means of alleviating them.

Fortunately, when it comes to psychological disorders, knowing the facts is a giant step toward solving the problems.

CHAPTER 1

SUICIDE: THE FACTS

In the painting Lucretia and Tarquinius, the Italian painter Titian (ca. 1488–1576) uses dark tones to portray the tragic suicide of Lucretia. Renowned for her beauty and virtue, she stabbed herself after being raped.

Suicide is the eighth leading cause of death in the United States. Approximately 35,000 suicides are reported annually, but experts suggest that 100,000 may be a truer figure because so many suicides are officially ruled as accidents. Reports indicate that suicide attempts reach much higher numbers: It is estimated that 5 million people now living in the United States have attempted suicide.

Suicide statistics for younger people are particularly disturbing: Once every 80 seconds, an adolescent attempts to take his or her own life; once every 100 minutes, 1 succeeds. Each year, a recorded 5,000 young men and women between the ages of 15 and 24 die by suicide. Again, the true toll may include thousands more deaths that were officially ruled as accidents.

Tragically, the known suicide rate for young people has tripled since 1950. This not only matches the rate for other age groups but has also made suicide the third most common cause of death among teenagers, surpassed only by automobile accidents and murder. Yet the figures for teen suicide are not the only ones that have increased dramatically in recent years—the suicide rate among the elderly has also risen sharply. Thirteen out of every 100,000 young people aged 15 to 24 take their own life, compared to 22 out of every 100,000 people aged 75 to 84.

CIRCUMSTANCES SURROUNDING SUICIDE

What causes people to succumb to despair? Before examining other aspects of suicide, a look at some more statistics may offer clues to the

The years between 1970 and 1984 showed a marked increase in the percentage of young people using firearms to commit suicide; that trend continues today.

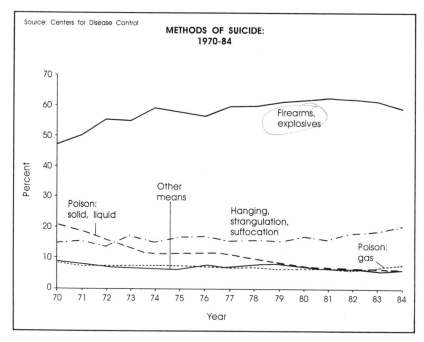

circumstances surrounding it. Moreover, by examining causes and questioning misconceptions associated with suicide, friends and family members become better equipped to prevent it.

This is particularly important because the actual suicidal crisis lasts a very short time—usually about 10 minutes. If a person considering suicide can be helped through that period, the desire may weaken.

METHODS

Statistics show that males have a much higher rate of suicide than females. Although females are three times more likely than males to attempt suicide, males succeed more often: Out of every five people who actually commit suicide, approximately four are male.

Men typically use faster and more violent methods, such as guns, to end their life, whereas women frequently use drugs and can often be

Access to firearms makes suicide easier—and more certain. Although fewer men than women attempt suicide, three times as many men actually die because they are more likely to use guns.

saved with medical treatment. However, according to the book *Coping with Suicide* by Judie Smith, 55% of all teens who commit suicide use guns. The teenage girls who died from a suicide attempt were more likely to have used a gun than to have taken drugs or slashed their wrists.

Another study, published in the *American Journal of Public Health* in 1986, reported that between 1933 and 1982 the suicide rates involving firearms increased 3 times faster than any other means of suicide among 15 to 19 year olds; it increased 10 times faster among 20 to 24 year olds.

SEASONS OF SUICIDE

Contrary to popular belief, the largest number of suicides does not occur during holiday seasons. Many people believe that the Thanksgiving and Christmas holidays bring on despair in people who feel lonely, yet more suicides occur in the spring—particularly in May. Researchers suggest that this may be due to the general sense of rebirth and coming to life associated with the season. Severely depressed individuals, lacking a personal sense of rebirth, may feel at odds with the world in general. This feeling may confirm a person's decision to take his or her own life.

Another widely held belief—that most suicides occur in the middle of the night—also is not supported by available data. Many suicides actually occur during daylight hours. Some researchers suggest that although many depressed people manage to make it through a long night of questioning and despair, the breakthrough of the sun—again, a sort of rebirth—may strengthen their resolve to commit suicide. This theory is similar to that of why suicides increase in the spring.

SUICIDE IN SOCIETY

Most people are not aware of how widely pervasive suicide has become, but in truth, it has reached epidemic proportions in the United

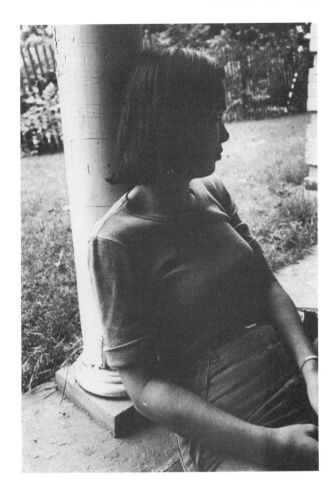

Teenagers are especially susceptible to feelings of despair when they encounter difficulties with which they have not yet learned to cope.

States. In some parts of the country, and in certain age groups, the number of suicides has even surpassed the regional homicide rate.

No specific group of people or type of person is easily defined as suicidal. Indeed, many suicides occur because people could not believe a friend or family member was the suicidal "type." However, three feelings, familiar to all people at one time or another, eventually overwhelm those who attempt suicide: loss, loneliness, and hopelessness.

A prevalent attitude that adds to the problems surrounding suicide is the social taboo against it. Because so many people see it as shameful, a person who is considering suicide may not want to discuss his or her thoughts openly. This causes people who feel depressed and alone to imagine themselves to be even more isolated. Furthermore, if family members or friends of someone who is contemplating suicide are reluctant to talk about it, they may miss an opportunity to help prevent the tragedy. Finally, social stigma often makes recovery more difficult for those who survive the suicide of a loved one.

CHAPTER 2

SUICIDE IN HISTORY

Émile Durkheim (1858–1917), a pioneer in the field of sociology, introduced the scientific study of suicide and its causes at the beginning of the 20th century.

Suicide is not a new phenomenon. Yet the topic was not examined scientifically until 1897, when pioneer sociologist Émile Durkheim published his revolutionary book *Suicide: A Study in Sociology*. In this work, Durkheim suggested that suicide rates increase when a society's value system breaks down. Despite science's late introduction to the subject, evidence from both art and literature suggests that despair and the resulting urge to take one's own life have existed throughout the centuries—in every civilization and culture.

BIBLICAL SUICIDE

pro

Many of the earliest recordings of suicide occur in the Bible. Of those, the best known is probably that of Judas, who betrayed Jesus. According to the New Testament, Judas was so distraught over his actions that he hanged himself.

The suicide of Samson is noted in the Old Testament. Before he was conceived, an angel visited Samson's mother to foretell his birth. The angel warned that as long as his hair was not cut, Samson would deliver Israel from the Philistines, a rival nation that had been enslaving the Israelites. However, Samson eventually succumbed to the wiles of Delilah.

He revealed the secret source of his strength to her, but she betrayed him. Once his hair was cut, the Philistines blinded him, rendering him helpless. Samson, however, regained his strength and wreaked vengeance by bringing a temple crashing down upon himself and the enemy.

con

The Catholic church has condemned suicide as a sin since the time of St. Augustine in the 5th century. Suicide was officially banned by the Council of Braga in A.D. 563, when the Catholic clergy declared that it broke the sixth commandment—Thou shalt not kill. Followers believed, in fact, that suicide was the ultimate sin.

con

Today, Judaism, Christianity, and most other religions in the world consider suicide morally wrong. The more a religion opposes suicide,

Sixteenth-century Flemish artist Pieter Brueghel the Elder (ca. 1525–69) depicts The Suicide of Saul (1562), the first king of Israel, who led his people to many victories over the Philistines but killed himself after a major defeat and loss of honor.

the less likely its members are to take their own life. By the same token, the more religious a person is, the less chance there is that he or she will commit suicide.

Throughout the centuries, suicides have been treated differently than deaths by natural causes. During medieval times, people who took their own life were denied burial in sacred ground by the Catholic church. Others were buried only at crossroads or left unburied. Yet there have also been times throughout history when suicide was viewed as proper and even heroic.

SUICIDE ACROSS CULTURES

During World War II, the Allies watched in fear as Japanese bomber pilots sacrificed their lives to hit their targets. These *kamikaze* pilots, who flew suicide missions, were considered national heroes. The young men accepted to this attack corps felt that dying for their country was a great honor. As such, suicide was viewed as justifiable.

Two more examples of socially acceptable suicide are the Japanese practice of *hara-kiri* and the Hindu custom of *suttee*. Hara-kiri—ritual self-disembowelment—was performed to protect one's honor. Warriors committed hara-kiri to avoid being taken prisoner and possibly betraying their country.

Until recently, Suttee was an accepted suicide ritual in India and is probably still practiced in some outlying areas. Followers of Hinduism burn their dead on funeral pyres rather than bury them, and a wife was expected to throw herself over her husband's burning body as a final display of love and respect. Hindus believed that the woman, burned alive, would then proceed into the next life with her husband.

HISTORICAL FIGURES

Suicide has affected both the famous and the infamous. Not only has it impacted history, but it has also silenced artists who, had they chosen to live, might have continued to give the world the benefit of their genius.

SUICIDE: POLITICAL OR PERSONAL?

Although it is possible to identify the causes of suicide for specific victims, the task becomes more difficult when looking for risk factors encompassing entire nations. It has been found, however, that countries with higher suicide rates do have certain cultural characteristics in common.

In the past, it has been suggested that the environment created by some types of political systems actually increases the potential for suicide. But sociologists have since taken a closer look at a variety of factors and found that culture has a far greater impact than do politics. Similar types of cultural experiences or values, running far deeper in a society than political views, can exist in very different types of political systems. Examples include the following:

- A dramatic event that seems to threaten an individual's happiness or the nation's future. The passing of a national hero can be a traumatic event. For instance, some young people have been known to commit suicide after learning of the death of an idol, such as an actor or a singer.

- A lack of people or institutions to provide emotional support. A comparison of suicide rates among countries with strong family values illustrates the importance of such support. Italian, Irish, and Norwegian families typically offer a great deal of support to children both in their early years and later in life. All of these cultures are known to have lower suicide rates than those with less supportive families. In Denmark, where the suicide rate is high, both parents usually work away from home during the child's formative years, and extended families are less significant.

- Cultural attitudes toward suicide. Statistics indicate that countries with negative attitudes toward suicide (for example, Norway) have lower suicide rates than do nations with less negative views (such as Denmark).

- Strong pressure for individuals to display excellence. This demand is particularly damaging in countries in which people are judged by the success of their career. For instance, young people in Japan face immense pressure to compete for university admittance, taking an entrance test that will affect their career and the rest of their life. The apparent result of such stress is an extremely high teen suicide rate.

THE CASE OF JAPAN

All four of the cultural risk factors listed prevail in Japan, producing what appears to be a fertile ground for suicide. The effort to enter a good university produces two of the previously described situations in the life of many Japanese youths: an extremely dramatic event and the demand to succeed.

In Japan, success in a career is extremely important, yet such success is based entirely on other people's judgment and approval. The test that determines admittance to a university becomes a crucial factor in a young person's life. The arrival of the test scores marks a dramatic moment, and a failure to do well may cause a drastic reaction.

Moreover, lack of emotional support affects young people in Japan. Unlike in the West, where suicide rates generally increase with age, in Japan the rates peak both among young people and the elderly. In 1988, the suicide rate for those aged 75 and over was 65.5%; for the age group 15 to 24 it was 10.3%. Interestingly, the Japanese teen suicide rate has decreased since 1983, when it was 11.8%, making the 1988 U.S. teen suicide rate higher than that of Japan.

As Japanese culture changes, teenagers are caught in a struggle to accept modern values but may have difficulty coping with traditional customs. This cultural upheaval creates an atmosphere in which many young people believe that their views are misunderstood or unacceptable. They may interpret these differences of opinion as personal rejection.

Additionally, Japanese society has viewed suicide as an acceptable way to die for thousands of years. Hence, there is no cultural stigma that might help prevent suicide. For example, the president of one Japanese company that manufactured a food product that accidentally poisoned consumers committed suicide out of a sense of responsibility for the company's error. This is not an unusual occurrence: 275 company directors killed themselves in 1986.

All of these factors are part of an integral belief system in Japan and other nations. However, if families strive to create a strong support system, they can do much to overcome an individual's urge to take his or her own life.

Cleopatra (69–30 B.C.), the last Egyptian queen of the Ptolemy dynasty, chose to die from the bite of a poisonous snake rather than surrender Egypt to the Roman Empire.

The defeat and disgrace of war has long proved a trigger for suicide. More than 2,000 years ago, the Egyptian queen Cleopatra arranged to be bitten by an asp (a poisonous snake) rather than allow herself to be taken prisoner following Rome's victory over her army. The most infamous character to commit suicide in this century was German dictator Adolf Hitler. In 1945, with his Third Reich in ruins and defeat by Allied forces imminent, he and his companion, Eva Braun, took poison in their bunker in Berlin.

Even in peaceful times, the past 100 years alone have seen the self-destruction of a number of great artists. The Dutch painter Vincent van Gogh, who used broad brushstrokes and intense colors to develop his own Expressionist style, shot himself in 1890. Despite his legendary status today, he lived unappreciated and in poverty, circumstances

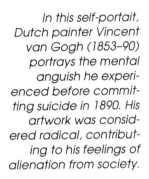
In this self-portait, Dutch painter Vincent van Gogh (1853–90) portrays the mental anguish he experienced before committing suicide in 1890. His artwork was considered radical, contributing to his feelings of alienation from society.

made worse by his bouts with depression and loneliness. In 1932, American poet Hart Crane jumped overboard while traveling from Mexico to New York by steamer. Although Crane, author of the epic poem *The Bridge*, did enjoy some success during his life, he was high-strung and eventually unable to cope with the death of his father, mounting financial difficulties, his own alcoholism, and his inability to write a long-planned work.

British writer Virginia Woolf, famous for her experimental techniques, suffered several nervous breakdowns during her lifetime. Fearing another collapse, she drowned herself in 1941. Two decades later, Ernest "Papa" Hemingway, author of such classic novels as *The Sun Also Rises* and *For Whom the Bell Tolls*, grew fearful that he could not write another great book. This, along with his failing health, apparently contributed to Hemingway's decision to commit suicide. The writer placed a hunting rifle in his mouth and pulled the trigger. A year later, Marilyn Monroe, Hollywood's blond bombshell, was found dead from an overdose of barbiturates. Although some people believe Monroe's

Perhaps America's best-known author of this century, Ernest Hemingway (1899–1961), was admired for his short stories and novels. However, he became depressed later in life and shot himself in 1961.

death was murder, many more accept it as suicide. She had long suffered from problems with drugs and mental illness.

American writer Sylvia Plath, author of the novel *The Bell Jar* and a number of poetry collections, also suffered from deep emotional problems. She initially attempted suicide during her adolescence and took her own life in 1963.

A type of cultural despair was apparently behind the suicide of Japanese writer Yukio Mishima. The author committed hara-kiri in

Japanese author Yukio Mishima (1925–70) enacts the ritual suicide of hara-kiri in his self-written and -directed film Yukoku. He later committed suicide as a protest against the Japanese government for giving up too many ancient traditions.

1970 in protest against creeping Western influence in his country as well as what he considered to be Japan's military weakness.

Perhaps the most shocking example of suicide in the 20th century occurred in 1978, when more than 900 members of the People's Temple apparently took their own life. The sect was founded by Jim Jones, who persuaded the families to leave the United States and form a colony in a remote area of Guyana, a South American country. When their journey to find a better way of life proved unsuccessful, Jones instructed his followers to commit suicide. The group, including parents, their children, and Jones himself, ingested poison-laced punch and then lay down to die under the brutal sun.

SUICIDE IN ART

In literature, Shakespeare is well known for his tragedies involving suicide. The famous speech that begins, "To be or not to be . . ."

This 1852 work by Sir John Everett Millais (1829–96) portrays Ophelia, a character who goes insane and eventually drowns herself after learning of her father's death, in Shakespeare's Hamlet.

expresses the thoughts of Hamlet, the young prince of Denmark, as he contemplates suicide. Yet, in *Hamlet*, Ophelia is actually the grief-stricken character who jumps into a river and drowns after learning of her father's death.

Perhaps Shakespeare's best-known suicide—in fact, a double suicide—is that of Romeo and Juliet. Separated by their families and forbidden to love each other, Juliet feigns death by drinking a sleeping potion, planning to later awaken in her tomb and run off in secret with Romeo. Circumstances, however, go tragically awry when Romeo, arriving too soon and mistakenly believing that Juliet is dead, poisons himself and dies beside her. Upon awakening, Juliet discovers what has happened and plunges Romeo's dagger into her breast, taking her own life.

Unfortunately, stories such as this tend to romanticize suicide. Young people, in particular, may be susceptible to the idea of this "glamorous" type of demise. However, it takes more than mere stories to create thoughts of suicide. In fact, any number of problems or difficult circumstances, as well as chemical and biological imbalances, can drive a person to the brink of despair.

CHAPTER 3

CAUSES AND RISK FACTORS

Shakespeare's play Romeo and Juliet *is so well known for the suicide of its young lovers that one modern expert coined the phrase* "Romeo and Juliet Factor" *to describe suicides provoked by romantic difficulties.*

Circumstances that predispose a person to consider or commit suicide are known as *risk factors*. Uncovering these factors has taken extensive, ongoing research, but understanding them enables mental health counselors, as well as communities in general, to focus their energy on helping people who seem more vulnerable to suicide. Risk factors range from childhood difficulties to personal problems to chemical imbalances.

PSYCHOLOGICAL FACTORS

Domestic stress, often stemming from a broken home or abusive parents or partners, is a major risk factor for suicide. Teens are particularly vulnerable because they may not be able to deal with divorce, stepparents, or stepsiblings. (Interestingly, married people have the lowest risk of suicide.)

In addition, children of parents experiencing problems such as depression or substance abuse, or who have attempted suicide themselves, are more likely to try to take their own life. According to a 1984 study by epidemiologist Myrna Weissman of Columbia University (reported in the *Journal of the American Academy of Child Psychiatry*), of the subjects whose parents had suffered from depression, 6.5% exhibited suicidal thoughts. However, suicidal thoughts rarely occurred among people whose parents had not been seriously depressed.

Early traumas, such as physical, sexual, or psychological abuse, can cause a child to feel deprived, rejected, or unloved and can develop into anger and resentment in a teenager. These emotions may lead to feelings of guilt and, eventually, to self-destructive behavior.

Researchers Michael L. Peck, Ph.D., and Robert E. Litman, M.D., investigated recent trends in teenage suicide and discovered that approximately 90% of suicidal young people felt that their family did not understand them. Moreover, two-thirds of those who committed suicide had reportedly been on bad terms with their family. Many of them had been unable to express feelings of frustration and failure to their parents, who reacted with denial or hostility. The parents themselves tended to be extremely driven to succeed and to possess their own excessive insecurities and fear of failure.

In addition, teens living under the pressure of high expectations can suffer a great deal of stress. Often, a person who tries to live up to someone else's expectations or sets extremely high standards for him- or herself may feel that there is no way to avoid failure, so that even a minor setback can seem completely humiliating.

Once someone is feeling depressed or overwhelmed by life's disappointments and difficulties, a new crisis may cause a sudden suicidal reaction. This can include problems with school or the law, a move to

Native Americans—an ethnic group often caught in a desperate cycle of poverty—have the highest rate of suicide in the United States.

a new home, the breakup of a romance, divorce in the family, unplanned pregnancy, or the illness of a loved one.

The size of one's peer group may also add stress by increasing competition. In 1988, the *American Psychiatric Press Review of Psychiatry* published an article revealing that the suicide rate among 15 to 24 year olds has historically fluctuated in proportion to the size of that age group within the population. The greater the percentage of the population within that age group, the greater the suicide rate among them tends to become.

In the United States, the black population, like the Native American population, is plagued by a low standard of living. The rate of attempted suicides among blacks is particularly high.

31

Statistics also indicate that certain groups of people are more prone to kill themselves. As mentioned, although more women than men attempt suicide, more men succeed. In addition, a higher percentage of blacks than Caucasians attempt suicide, but more Caucasians actually kill themselves. Compared to other ethnic groups, Native Americans, long believed to have one of the highest alcoholism and substance abuse rates in the United States, also have the highest suicide rate.

Other groups that have high suicide rates include the severely or chronically ill. In recent years, the number of suicides among AIDS victims has risen. AIDS (acquired immune deficiency syndrome) is an often fatal disease that breaks down the body's immune system and leaves it unable to fight off infection and illness. AIDS, a contagious disease that is greatly affecting the homosexual community, is probably the cause of the rise in the homosexual suicide rate. AIDS and other fatal diseases, such as cancer, are often viewed as inevitable death sentences to those diagnosed with them.

People in certain high-stress jobs, such as policemen, lawyers, and health care professionals (including doctors, nurses, psychiatrists, counselors, and dentists), are also at a higher risk for suicide. People who are "loners" (those without a social network) may be predisposed

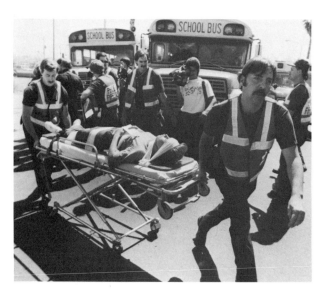

People who have chosen certain high-stress careers, including health care and law enforcement, have been found to have an especially high suicide rate.

to suicide as well. In addition, individuals who have previously attempted suicide are at much greater risk to try again than those who have not. In fact, four out of five people who commit suicide have attempted it at least once before.

Some risk factors also serve as warning signs that a person is considering suicide. They include alcohol and substance abuse, loss of a loved one, or a suicide committed by someone close. These will be discussed in Chapter 4.

BIOLOGICAL FACTORS

For years people assumed that only mental or emotional problems drove people to commit suicide. Scientists have now begun to explore possible physical causes as well and have uncovered some disturbing information. A variety of recent studies suggest a number of physical factors that can increase a person's tendency to commit suicide.

In a study conducted by Drs. Neal D. Ryan and Joaquim Puig-Antich of the University of Pittsburgh, physiological differences were discovered between adolescents who had planned or attempted suicide and their "normal" peers. The adolescents who considered suicide had much lower levels of growth hormone. Produced by the pituitary gland, growth hormone plays a role in bone and muscle development, and its deficiency may indicate a serious physical problem.

Other studies have shown that people who use violent methods to kill themselves have a much lower level of the neurotransmitter *serotonin* in their brain. (A neurotransmitter is a chemical messenger that carries impulses throughout the body.) The function of serotonin is not entirely known, but recent research links it to sleep, sensory perception, and depression.

Traumatic Births

Another researcher, Dr. Lee Salk, a psychologist and professor at Cornell University Medical School in New York, believes that traumatic or difficult birth experiences put certain people at a much higher risk for suicide.

HEAVY METAL SUICIDE

How powerful is the music that young people listen to? This question has come up often in the past decade, especially as heavy metal music, which often features lyrics containing destructive or violent imagery, has gained popularity. As more young people listen to this music, a growing number of parents have begun to feel that heavy metal is very powerful indeed—powerful enough to kill. Two famous cases have brought heavy metal rockers to court under the accusation that their songs drove teenagers to commit suicide.

The first case was that of Judas Priest, a heavy metal group from Britain that released the album *Stained Class* in 1978. Two days before Christmas in 1985, 19-year-old James Vance and 18-year-old Raymond Belknap had been listening to the album for several hours while drinking a large amount of beer. Then they went out to the cemetery of their Nevada town and took turns using the same shotgun. Belknap killed himself, but Vance's suicide attempt managed only to destroy his face. (Although he sur-vived that attempt, Vance took his own life three years later.)

Afterward, the families of both boys sued Judas Priest and CBS Records, which distributed *Stained Class*, claiming that the album contained subliminal messages encouraging listeners to commit suicide. The case did go to trial, but the court ruled in favor of the band's right of free speech.

Nevertheless, the parents continued the case with an appeal. On August 24, 1990, a judge ruled that the band was not intentionally sending subliminal messages to encourage suicide. He also ruled that no scientific evidence existed to suggest that subliminal messages could cause someone to attempt suicide.

In 1986, a similar suit was filed against another British heavy metal rocker, Ozzy Osbourne, after 19-year-old John Mc-Collum, Jr., killed himself with a shotgun blast. The boy's father blamed his son's death on Osbourne's song "Suicide Solu-tion," but as in the earlier case the court upheld Osbourne's right of free speech.

John McCollum holds the Ozzy Osbourne album containing the song "Suicide Solution," which he believes led his 19-year-old son John, Jr., to shoot himself. Although the song actually has an anti-suicide message, this father—like many parents in recent years—feels that heavy metal music affects young people in a negative way.

Cases such as these have fueled the fire of a group called the Parent's Music Resource Centre. Led by Tipper Gore, wife of Tennessee senator Albert Gore, Jr., the group is fighting against sex and violence in music. They have proposed legislation that would require albums to have stickers warning consumers if the album contains explicit lyrics. However, this system has gone into effect in very few states.

Meanwhile, opponents of the parents group argue that the war against teenage suicide starts at home. They believe that better communication between parents and teenagers is the most important deterrent to the problem. They recommend that parents become more aware of what their children watch on television and listen to on the radio. In the Judas Priest case, they also point out that the two teenagers involved had both lived tragic lives. Each boy had grown up in a broken home with abusive parents, and both boys had continually abused drugs. Such sad stories indicate that the teens' problems began long before they started listening to heavy metal music.

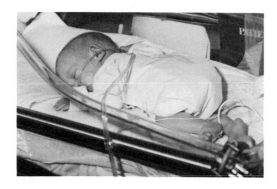

Scientific studies indicate that babies who suffer respiratory difficulty during or shortly after birth may be more prone to suicidal tendencies later in life.

Salk began his research by studying neonatal intensive care units, special nurseries that care for ill or undersized newborns. According to a November 1988 article in *Omni* magazine, he noted that more babies were being saved with newer, more sophisticated medical equipment, yet in the following years, suicide rates were also rising.

Salk reported, "The infant mortality rate began dropping substantially around fifteen years before we started seeing an increase in teenage suicide rates." Salk wondered if the two were connected, noting, "Males suffer from more birth complications than females do, and they kill themselves more often."

To test his hypothesis, Salk studied the birth records of 52 individuals born between 1957 and 1967, all of whom had been teenage suicide victims. He then compared those statistics to a *control group* of 104 young people born within the same period, none of whom had committed suicide. (Control groups are used in scientific experiments to compare a "typical" group to the one being researched in order to ensure that the results are unbiased and accurate.) After comparing the data, Salk discovered 3 characteristics that stood out in those who had committed suicide: being born to a mother who received little or no prenatal care during the first 20 weeks of her pregnancy; being born to a mother who suffered from chronic disease throughout the pregnancy; or having experienced respiratory difficulties for at least 1 hour after birth.

Although close to 20% of births in the United States involve at least one of these factors, Salk estimates that 60% of the adolescents who commit suicide have been through such trauma. According to Salk's theory, a baby who suffers respiratory distress for more than one hour

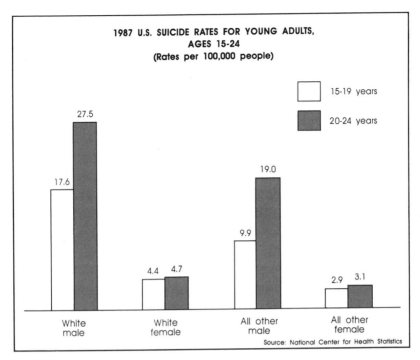

1987 U.S. SUICIDE RATES FOR YOUNG ADULTS, AGES 15-24
(Rates per 100,000 people)

☐ 15-19 years

■ 20-24 years

27.5

19.0

17.6

9.9

4.4 4.7

2.9 3.1

White male   White female   All other male   All other female

Source: National Center for Health Statistics

Studies of the 1987 death rates indicate a high rate of male suicides compared to female suicides. In the United States, 72% of all suicides are carried out by white males.

after birth may have sustained some neurological damage that can impair his or her ability to deal with the stresses of life. Additionally, those babies who have "died" of such complications and been medically brought back to life may have "a diminished fear of death."

The other two factors, while seemingly biological, probably have a deeper basis in emotions. A mother who has not sought early prenatal care may not want to have a baby. Consequently, as the child grows older, he or she may sense this and feel outcast. On the other hand, a very ill mother may not have the strength to raise a child and may instead direct all her energy toward her own recovery.

Means of Death

Another scientist, Dr. Bertil Jacobson of Stockholm's Karolinska Institute, reinforced Salk's findings and made another startling discovery as well. These risk factors may influence not only the urge to commit suicide, he found, but also the way in which it is attempted.

In a study conducted in Sweden, Jacobson found that individuals who had killed themselves by hanging, strangulation, drowning, or carbon monoxide poisoning were more than four times as likely to have suffered oxygen deprivation at birth than individuals in the control group. Of those who used a more mechanical means to commit suicide—such as jumping from a bridge or building or shooting or cutting themselves—20% had suffered a difficulty at birth deemed mechanical, including a *breech* presentation or a delay requiring forceps delivery. (A breech birth occurs when the baby's feet or buttocks appear first. To prevent complications, doctors often perform a surgical delivery called a cesarean section. Forceps are tonglike instruments used to guide a baby through the birth canal.)

Jacobson has also suggested that the administration of certain drugs (such as opiates, barbiturates, or chloroform) to the mother during labor may lead to drug addiction later in the child's life. The researcher noted that clusters of people who had been born in certain hospitals in Stockholm were becoming addicts later in life. He theorized that these babies, born in hospitals where doctors were more likely to administer such drugs, were highly susceptible to addiction.

How can birth experiences have such deep, long-term effects? Jacobson believes that human beings may have some sort of imprinting reflex, similar to that of other animals, that engraves these experiences on their memory for life. Psychologist David B. Chamberlain of San Diego, California, has a different theory. According to a November 1988 article in *Omni*, Chamberlain believes that traumatic birth experiences are "carried within the body on some kind of cellular level," suggesting a physical, rather than mental, condition.

Even if difficult experiences at birth are a major risk factor for suicide, there are many other elements that may predispose a person to take his or her life. Being aware of the warning signs may help avoid tragedy.

CHAPTER 4

WARNING SIGNS AND MYTHS

Suicide has become a growing problem among the elderly, who often find themselves alone after the death of a loved one.

There were so many things I kept asking myself after Katherine committed suicide. I wondered if I were in some way responsible—I hadn't seen her in a while and I wondered if I simply hadn't been there when she needed me. And then there was a part of me that couldn't understand how she could've done what she'd done—that couldn't believe that things had been that bad. That's when all of us—her friends—began to look back and put the pieces of the puzzle together. It seemed like each of us had a different piece, and together they formed a picture of someone who really needed help—who had a lot of problems that no one could've suspected or even begun to deal with. Afterward, we realized that we had gone a long way toward answering the question why.

—Jennifer, 17, a close friend of Katherine's

When someone has attempted or committed suicide, friends and family members are often left with nothing but questions. Was there something I could have done? Was I too hard on him or her? Were there any signals—did I miss them? Perhaps the most common question of all is Why?

In some cases there are simply no answers—no indications of trouble, no signs that anything had been disturbing the victim. These

This Colorado man, distressed over his inability to find work, consented to be returned to safety only after being offered a job.

cases, however, are rare. In fact, research indicates that four out of five suicides are preceded by some sort of symptom. The majority of people who take their own life leave a visible trail of despair—broken relationships, trouble at home or school, problems with the law, a history of substance abuse, or declining health and advanced age.

WARNING SIGNS

Signals of an impending suicide are often cries for help—a last attempt to reach out. Warning signs include

- a preoccupation with suicide or death. A person thinking about suicide may question friends about different methods or perhaps show an unusual interest either in guns or in learning the size of a lethal dose of sleeping pills. The individual may repeatedly discuss other suicides, particularly that of someone close, or plan his or her own funeral and make final wishes known to people. He or she may also frequently discuss the subject of death.

- gallows humor. A person may also begin joking about suicide, making light of the matter. Yet that individual

The suicide rate among AIDS patients continues to rise as incidence of the disease increases. In recent decades, terminal illness has spawned heated debate in medical and legal circles. Many terminally ill patients believe their doctors should be allowed to comply with their wish to die.

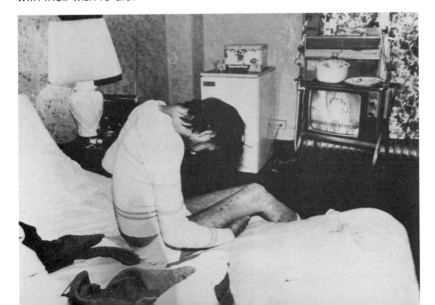

is often paying close attention to others' reactions to these seemingly casual remarks.

- tying up loose ends or putting affairs in order. An individual contemplating suicide often clears his or her schedule, finishes up projects, and gives away belongings.

- knowing someone who recently committed suicide. Young people who had a friend who committed suicide may be obsessed with their friend's death and be at a somewhat greater risk for suicide themselves. The grief over having a friend die can seem overwhelming, and suicide may appear to present a way out. In addition, after seeing so many mourners and hearing all of the wonderful things that were said about the deceased, suicide may come to seem like a glamorous way to die and rejoin the friend.

- depression. A depressed person may suffer from low self-esteem and feelings of worthlessness as well as from a loss of hope. This type of person is susceptible to the idea of suicide as an escape route from all the seemingly insurmountable problems he or she must face. An individual who appears withdrawn, with little interest in events or people that normally attract his or her attention, may be considering suicide. Depression that persists beyond the normal blue period that everyone sometimes experiences may be a sign that professional help is needed.

- insomnia, sleep disturbances, and eating problems, such as anorexia and disinterest in food. A person suffering from these problems may exhibit signs of fatigue, weakness, dizziness, and even physical numbness. Physical troubles such as severe headaches or prolonged illnesses may lead an individual to contemplate suicide as an escape from the pain.

- poor grooming. A person considering suicide may neglect his or her appearance, wearing dirty or rumpled clothing and leaving his or her hair unwashed. An individual who has always been fastidious may suddenly start to wear the same clothes for days on end or neglect to bathe.

- poor grades. An adolescent contemplating suicide may begin failing in school, lose interest in extracurricular activities or friends, or become belligerent or apathetic in the classroom. Homework assignments may be left undone, as the teen planning to take his or her own life decides that there is no point in continuing an education.

- indifference to an "accident." If an individual seems to care little about a mishap in which he or she was involved, even if that person suffered great physical injury, this may indicate that the episode was an attempt to commit suicide through reckless behavior.

- radical personality change. Children who were once obedient and calm may become defiant and excitable. Competent professionals may become slipshod or preoccupied. A person who has always been nervous and high-strung may become very calm and accepting before taking his or her own life. One of the most serious signs of impending suicide occurs when a person who has been depressed for a long time suddenly cheers up and displays unusual resolve. Often, this individual has

Emotional pain caused by the loss of a loved one may lead surviving friends or family members to consider suicide. When their son Joshua accidentally drowned, Diane and George Mendenhall were so grieved that they took their own life.

A CONTROVERSIAL QUESTION: THE RIGHT TO DIE

On a Monday in June 1989, Janet Adkins climbed into the back of a van in the parking lot of a state park in Michigan, lay down, and with no more effort than it took to press a button, ended her life and set off a national furor over the right to die. The 54-year-old schoolteacher from Oregon had become the first person to use a "suicide machine," an invention that injects a lethal drug into the bloodstream.

Invented by Dr. Jack Kevorkian, a retired pathologist, the suicide machine was Adkins's approach to death with dignity after learning that she was suffering from Alzheimer's disease, a terminal illness that slowly destroys its victim's memory. Still in the prime of life, Adkins was aware that her memory would soon begin to falter: She would first forget little details and then whole blocks of time. Eventually, her mind would be a blank slate, wiped clean of a lifetime's worth of memories, and she would become a burden to her family. Knowing this, Adkins preferred the alternative.

With Kevorkian monitoring her heart rate, she pushed a button on the machine, which pumped the drug into her body. Soon she was unconscious. In a short while, the compound reached her heart and Adkins died. Kevorkian immediately reported her death to the authorities.

Although suicide is not a crime in the state of Michigan, officials there decided to charge Kevorkian with murder for his part in Adkins's death. A judge found that there was no basis for the case, and all murder charges against him were dropped in December 1990. However, in a court decision on February 5, 1991, a circuit judge banned Kevorkian from using the machine again. Although Adkins was successful in her efforts, her death highlighted questions in the ongoing debate over the right to die: Should people be allowed to decide their own fate? Should ill patients be permitted to set limits for the amount and type of medical care they receive?

As medical research finds new ways to keep terminally ill patients alive longer, more and more people have begun to question their right to choose when to end treatment. To help achieve that end, many organizations now offer information on a *living*

The Hemlock Society takes its name from a plant used throughout the ages to produce a natural poison. This painting, The Death of Socrates, *portrays the famed Greek philosopher who was required to drink hemlock in 399 B.C. as a form of execution.*

will—a document instructing doctors and family members just how far to proceed with treatment. A living will can outline the removal of respirators and feeding tubes and when feeding should stop.

The most influential organization supporting the right to die movement is the Hemlock Society. Derek Humphry, an author who assisted his terminally ill wife in committing suicide, founded the organization in 1980.

Although Humphry is not legally able to offer advice about *euthanasia* (mercy killing) by speaking or writing to people directly, he discovered it is legal to produce a book for the general public. In 1987, he published *Let Me Die Before I Wake*, which he describes as "a suicide manual aimed at the terminally ill." That same year he also published a history of euthanasia entitled *The Right to Die*.

Some time earlier, Humphry put out the controversial book *Jean's Way*, which described his wife's death and his part in it. The book was one of the first to discuss euthanasia openly, and Humphry was overwhelmed with inquiries and requests for help from terminally ill patients and their families.

The Hemlock Society now has approximately 30,000 members nationwide, many of whom are elderly. Humphry feels the group's ultimate goal is to change legislation on a state-by-state basis so that the question of a patient's right to die is addressed. According to an article in the *Journal of Counseling and Development*, Humphry hopes that if his organization is successful, "dying people can ask their doctors to help them die; and, if the doctor wishes, he or she can hasten the end of that person without any legal liability."

decided to commit suicide and is experiencing relief at having finally made a decision.

CONTRIBUTING FACTORS

Drug abuse and alcohol problems often lead to or accompany a suicide attempt. For some people, diagnosis of a terminal illness is the crucial factor leading to suicide. A patient diagnosed with cancer or AIDS may choose to end his or her life before the disease does. This may explain why the suicide rate among AIDS victims is particularly high. Extremely painful diseases may provoke suicidal thoughts as well. For example, patients with bladder cancer, which is believed to be the most painful of all cancers, have a much higher suicide rate than do patients suffering from other types of the disease. For these people, the fear not only of excruciating pain but also of the loss of dignity often accompanies debilitating illness and is the deciding factor in taking their own life.

Among elderly people, the loss of a beloved spouse often gives rise to suicidal thoughts. The overwhelming grief of losing a partner can lead to deep despair, and suicide may be viewed both as a way to reunite with the deceased mate and as an escape from the pain of separation. Consequently, an elderly person who seems unable to cope with his or her grief and talks of "following" his or her spouse may be contemplating suicide.

MYTHS OF SUICIDE

A familiarity with the warning signs and risk factors of suicide is not always enough. A number of misconceptions surrounding suicide still exist that, if taken for fact, can be deadly. Some common myths include the following:

> *People who talk about committing suicide never actually go through with it.* This is perhaps the most dangerous of all misconceptions. A person who talks about suicide is thinking about it. He or she brings it up to test other people's reactions. Talking about suicide is actually a cry for help.

- *People who commit suicide always leave notes.* This is also not true. In fact, the majority of suicides do not leave notes. Many so-called accidents are mistakenly ruled as such because of the absence of a suicide note.

- *People who survive a suicide attempt never try again.* Actually, 80% of those who commit suicide have attempted to take their own life at least once before. (Repeat attempts often occur about three months after the person appears to have improved.) If problems have been severe enough to drive a person to try to take his or her own life, a failed attempt will not deter the individual from trying again—unless the problems have been solved.

- *Friends should not "tell" on a friend if he or she is talking about suicide.* This is particularly troubling to young people who do not want to betray a friend's

Thirteen-year-old Danny Holley hanged himself when he was unable to help solve his family's financial difficulties. A feeling of hopelessness is thought to be a key motive in suicides.

When an individual chooses to die rather than live with a government policy he or she finds intolerable, a political protest sometimes leads to suicide. Hunger strikes are one such form of protest; this Buddhist monk in Saigon, South Vietnam, chose another—death by fire.

confidence. No matter how angry the other person may become, however, a friend should always inform others of a possible suicide attempt. A parent, teacher, friend, or spouse may be able to get the troubled individual the help he or she needs.

/ *People should never mention the word suicide to someone who is already depressed.* An individual who is truly depressed may indeed be considering suicide, even if he or she has not mentioned it. Talking about suicide will not give a person the idea—in fact, it may show that someone cares enough to be concerned. Discussing the subject openly, even asking whether the person has considered suicide and what method he or she would use, may reveal just how seriously someone is thinking about it.

People who are seeing professional counselors never take their own life. A person who has sought professional help understands that he or she is unable to cope with certain problems alone. Too often, however, that individual grows even more despondent when, after a period of therapy, he or she is not cured. These unrealistic expectations cannot be met easily and may drive some people into a still deeper and seemingly unbeatable depression.

- *Suicides happen late at night.* Actually, most suicides occur during the day, as supported by a study conducted by Dr. Lucy Davidson and colleagues and reported in the November 17, 1989, issue of the *Journal of the American Medical Association.* Davidson's study of 14 suicides, in 2 separate clusters in Texas, concluded that none of the suicides took place between midnight and 6:00 A.M. In fact, 46% of the deaths occurred in the afternoon.

Young children never commit suicide. Today, more and more young people are taking their own life. There have been cases of preteen children killing themselves as well as reports of very young children—even preschoolers—who exhibit suicidal behavior.

- *People from good families never commit suicide.* Suicide claims people from all walks of life—rich and poor. Even individuals from seemingly perfect families are not immune. Many people, especially adolescents, derive a large part of their identity from their family. A family that is "perfect" may appear to leave no room for individual differences, and a member of such a household may begin to feel that it is impossible to ever be good enough. This is why many teens who are highly motivated take their own life after failing a test or having an encounter with the law, such as being caught shoplifting.

- *People who commit suicide are crazy.* Many people believe that only mentally ill people kill themselves. While this is true in some cases, it is not the rule. Many suicides are committed by people who are otherwise viewed as normal but cannot seem to find a way out of their current difficulties.

- *People who have attempted or thought about suicide remain suicidal for the rest of their life.* Though at a somewhat higher risk, many people who have attempted suicide go on to lead a normal, productive life. Some studies suggest that 70% of the general population has considered suicide at one time or another. Yet most people never go beyond that stage.

The Victim's Myth

Many people drawn to suicide are under the tragic misconception that taking their own life is a good form of revenge. These individuals imagine themselves looking down and having the last laugh on all the people with whom they are angry. They fail to realize that suicide means permanent loss, both for themselves and for the people who are left behind, devastated and numb with grief. Suicide does not get even with anyone.

CHAPTER 5

SUBSTANCE ABUSE AND DESTRUCTIVE BEHAVIOR

Reckless behavior is often overlooked as an expression of a death wish. These Lebanese soldiers are playing Russian roulette, which they call the Game of Death, with a pistol loaded with one round of live ammunition.

Bob is 19 years old. He has a steady job, a close family, and a girlfriend. He also has a problem with alcohol and drugs, mostly marijuana, and admits that he is dependent on them. Last year, one of Bob's close friends died in a suspicious accident that many people felt had really been suicide. Bob had a hard time dealing with his friend's death, and since then, he often seems preoccupied with suicide. Because his friend also battled unsuccessfully with substance abuse, Bob feels that death may be the only way to break free of his addiction.

When he is upset, or feels that things are not going his way, Bob threatens to slash his wrists or to "blow my brains out." "I'm better off dead," he is often heard saying.

At times Bob appears to be living on the edge—driving recklessly under the influence of alcohol or drugs. During these times, he tends to get upset more often, dwelling on the problems in his life. Although he has never attempted suicide, Bob's family is concerned that his destructive behavior is some sort of death wish and that his talk of suicide may be a cry for help. They have begged Bob to enter a rehabilitation program, such as Alcoholics Anonymous (AA), or to see a counselor. Bob, however, says he would rather die than do either of those things.

Cases such as Bob's are not unusual. Many young people behave recklessly, seeming to place little value on their own life. They drive too fast, drink too much, and take crazy chances. Fortunately, this risky behavior does not usually end fatally, but when it does, such deaths are often ruled as accidents.

In recent years, researchers have begun to question the accuracy of recorded suicide rates that do not take such fatalities into account.

The actual number of deaths due to suicide is unknown. Although many automobile accidents are the result of intoxication or reckless behavior, the circumstances may reveal an unspoken wish to die.

Annually, more than 44,000 people die in automobile accidents, and more than half of those accidents involve alcohol or a combination of psychoactive drugs. Thousands of other types of accidents also take place each year—drownings, overdoses, people hit by trains or falling from great heights—many of which involve drugs or alcohol and may, in truth, mask a suicide. Indeed, many suicide attempts take place while an individual is under the influence of a psychoactive substance—one that chemically alters the mind and behavior.

ALCOHOL

Although few people think of it as such, alcohol is a drug, albeit a legal one, and it is no less dangerous than other drugs. Many people drink to relax or to drop inhibitions, but alcohol's reputation as "the life of the party" is erroneous. Although it may at first appear to elevate mood, alcohol is in fact a depressant. Consuming even two or three drinks will affect one's ability to reason; impair one's coordination, speech, vision, and sense of balance; and cause a loss of self-control.

Alcohol is a crucial factor in many suicides. As in the case of this Boston woman, some people who are inebriated may become convinced that dangerous behavior will not harm them. It may also give them courage to follow through with a suicide attempt without fear of the consequences.

In this state, a person's emotions are often magnified. If an individual is already depressed, he or she may become even more so after inhibitions and self-control are lowered. Consequently, if a person was having suicidal thoughts before he or she began drinking, those feelings may become overwhelming. In this individual's hands, a car may become a weapon of self-destruction, which leads many researchers to question whether many of the one-car accidents that occur each year are, indeed, accidental.

NONALCOHOLIC DRUGS

Sedative drugs, such as marijuana, are often used in combination with alcohol. These drugs not only compound the effects of alcohol but in high concentrations also cause hallucinations. Among adolescents and young adults, alcohol and marijuana are the two most widely abused substances, both alone and in combination.

Other drugs commonly abused include stimulants, or speed, such as cocaine and amphetamines. These are used to speed up actions and produce a high. Unfortunately, these drugs also give the user an exaggerated sense of self, sometimes leading him or her to feel invincible. In reality, the person's behavior becomes increasingly reckless as the drug's effects take hold. This in itself can lead to fatal accidents.

Although many people view drug use as a way to escape problems, drug abuse often ends fatally. Although alcohol has typically been the drug most associated with suicide, the increased use of crack and other dangerous drugs has caused the death rate among young people to rise.

Another downside to these drugs is the incredible low that follows the high. As the drug wears off, the user is left feeling particularly depressed. This can lead someone who is already depressed to deeper feelings of despondency as well as to thoughts of suicide. A chronic user can actually develop *cocaine psychosis*, an illness associated with high doses of cocaine that manifests itself in breaks from reality.

In addition, many adults are addicted to prescription drugs, including painkillers, sleeping pills, and muscle relaxants. While drugs alone may not prompt a person to take his or her life, prescription drugs can provide a suicidal person with a convenient method of self-destruction.

HARD EVIDENCE

While at one time most of the information linking substance abuse to suicide was pure speculation, recent studies conclude that chronic users of drugs and alcohol are at a higher risk for suicide than are nonusers. According to a study conducted by Charles L. Rich and associates at the State University of New York at Stony Brook and discussed in the June 18, 1988, issue of *Science News*, "Substance abusers . . . are more vulnerable to stress caused by 'interpersonal losses and conflicts.'" These losses can include losing a job, breaking up with a boyfriend or girlfriend, or having family problems.

Just as suicide rates have risen in the preteenage group, so have substance abuse rates. Pennsylvania's lieutenant governor Mark Singel (left) and secretary of health Dr. N. Mark Richards (right) look at a display designed to discourage alcohol abuse among 8 to 12 year olds.

The study, which included data from 283 suicides that took place in San Diego County, California, from 1981 to 1983, concluded that almost 60% of these suicides involved substance abusers. The study suggested that substance abusers between the ages of 20 and 30 were the ones most likely to take their own life following a personal loss; 42% of the suicides in that age group who had been drug or alcohol abusers had recently suffered such a tragedy, as compared to 38% in those over 30.

Drug use also varies according to age. The Stony Brook study found that the drug most commonly abused by suicide victims, particularly among older subjects, was alcohol. Younger people who took their own life more frequently abused marijuana, cocaine, amphetamines, or various combinations of these drugs; alcohol was also often involved.

Furthermore, the subjects had been struggling with substance abuse problems for quite a while. Rich found that the average drug abuser who committed suicide had been using illicit drugs for close to 11 years, with or without alcohol. Alcoholics who committed suicide had, on average, suffered from an alcohol problem for 28 years. Oddly enough, Rich and his fellow researchers discovered that people with mood disorders, such as severe depression (a group already known to have an elevated risk of suicide), were less likely than substance abusers to take their life following a stressful event.

One researcher in the Stony Brook study, Dr. George E. Murphy of the Washington University School of Medicine in St. Louis, Missouri, recommended that professionals treating substance abusers keep a close lookout for any signs of depression or suicidal thoughts. He also suggested the implementation of a treatment program involving friends, family members, and perhaps hospitalization (for detoxification and close observation).

Although depression can make a person more susceptible to suicide, the results of the study suggest that substance abuse is a crucial added risk factor. Coupled with a mood disorder such as depression, substance abuse can easily take a fatal turn. To avoid this, treatment must deal both with the mood disorder and with the accompanying drug problem.

CHAPTER 6

PORTRAIT OF A SUICIDE

People who are depressed or confused often do not know where to turn for help. Friends should never be afraid to ask a troubled person if he or she is contemplating suicide. Open discussions are the first step toward solving seemingly insurmountable problems.

Caroline appeared to be an average 17 year old. She had long, shiny dark hair and a shy smile, and she lived with her family in an upper-middle-class neighborhood in a suburb of Philadelphia. She had a small but close group of friends and attended a private all-girl high school, where she made good grades.

Everything seemed to be going well for Caroline. She attended her first prom—her junior prom—and had a wonderful time. She danced all night, wearing a beautiful blue dress. Picking out the prom dress had meant a lot to Caroline—it was the first time she bought something to wear to such an important occasion. She looked great in the dress, too—all the pictures proved that. In every one, she was smiling, her eyes sparkling like stars. Toward the end of the summer, she seemed to be looking forward to returning to school, where she was going to be a senior—at the top of the heap for a change.

Caroline had other reasons to be happy, too. She had her first serious boyfriend and was looking into colleges, busily planning her future. Although earlier in the year she had been feeling pretty blue, Caroline seemed to have emerged from that period relatively unscathed. She appeared to be enjoying her time off with her friends and had made plans to get together with them for a big end-of-the-summer party. She never made it to the party, however. One week earlier, on a humid August afternoon, her parents returned home to find that their youngest child had locked herself in the garage, turned on the motor of her new car, lain down in the backseat, and died of carbon monoxide poisoning.

Although the names and places have been changed, Caroline's story is true. The following two interviews were conducted with Caroline's friends, eight years after her tragic death. This is just one example of how a suicide affects the lives of those who are left behind.

Anne, age 25: Caroline committed suicide over eight years ago, but sometimes I think back and it feels like only yesterday or last week. I remember how I first heard that Caroline was dead. I had just returned from seeing a movie with a friend when Marie called. We talked for a little while until my parents' phone started ringing downstairs. I asked Marie to hold on and ran down to answer the phone. It was another friend, Beth, and she sounded really shaky. She told me Caroline had committed suicide. We knew someone who had attempted suicide before, but to actually *kill* yourself seemed so unreal. I suppose a large part of me refused to grasp that Caroline was really dead. I kept thinking, Beth's upset over this, sure, but Caroline must be in the hospital somewhere recovering and she'll be fine. But, as we talked, it began to sink in.

After I hung up with Beth I knew I had to go back to my phone and tell Marie that Caroline was dead. They were close friends—I knew

Caroline confided in her more than in any other person—and I knew this would be devastating to her. When I told Marie that Caroline had committed suicide, she also had trouble grasping that Caroline was really gone. She kept sobbing and screaming into the phone, wanting to know how, and why—wanting to understand what happened. Other than knowing that Caroline was really dead, there was little else we knew for sure. After I hung up, I realized I was alone in the house—my parents were away—and suddenly I just had to be near someone. I stayed at a neighbor's for the rest of the weekend.

The next thing I remember is going to the wake. Hundreds of people were there—a lot of people we went to school with. At the time I thought it was strange that all of these people were there; most of them had little or nothing to do with Caroline other than attending some of the same classes. Looking back, it doesn't seem so strange. I guess we

From 1970 to 1987 in the United States, the annual rate of suicide did not change much overall. However, the number of suicides among 15 to 19 year olds rose substantially.

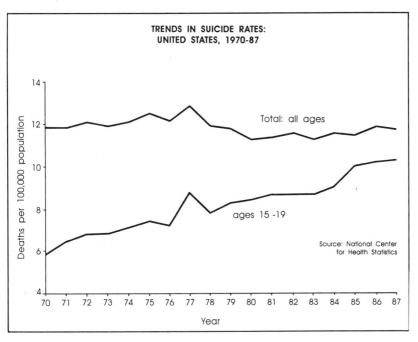

TRENDS IN SUICIDE RATES:
UNITED STATES, 1970-87

Total: all ages

ages 15 -19

Source: National Center
for Health Statistics

Deaths per 100,000 population

Year

were all so shocked that someone our age could actually be dead that attending the wake was one way of coming to terms with our own mortality.

At the wake, all I could think of was Caroline in the pictures from the junior prom—just a few short months before. Everything seemed so unreal. I remember everyone wondering whether or not the death would be ruled a suicide—a lot of people were questioning whether or not she would be granted a Christian burial, although no one knew for sure if the church still denied suicides burial in consecrated ground. The police finally ruled the death accidental. That was a great kindness to Caroline's parents, but now I think there must be a lot of other suicides ruled as accidental deaths. How real a picture can anyone get of the number of suicides in this country and of how many people really need help?

I didn't know what to say to Caroline's parents. Everything seemed inadequate. Oddly enough, they were comforting us. They told me how much I had meant to Caroline—little things she had told them. In some ways that made me feel better, but in others it made me feel worse. I hadn't seen Caroline in several weeks, and we hadn't even spoken for some time. On my part, I felt guilty—that I should have been there for her and wasn't, that I was more caught up in summer plans.

After the wake and the funeral, when things began to die down, I heard from Caroline's family. It was important to them to keep in touch with those people who had been her friends. I guess by keeping in touch with us, they were trying to hold on to a little of Caroline as well.

Several of us kept in touch with Caroline's parents for maybe a year afterward, but even then things were pretty strained. We knew we had to get on with our lives, and, as teenagers, there were so many other things to prepare for.

All of us were thinking about college and the senior prom, and that just reminded Caroline's parents that she would have been doing all this too. That's when I realized that as much as Caroline's death had affected all her friends, it had really devastated her parents. Although they joined support groups and came together as a family, Caroline's suicide left a void for them that was beyond comprehension.

Swiss painter Paul Klee (1879–1940) illustrates the confusion many people feel when they are unable to cope with life's hardships in his 1913 illustration Selbst Mörder Auf Der Brücke *(Suicide on the Bridge).*

My attitude toward people threatening suicide changed after Caroline's death. Maybe I worry too much when I hear someone say, "I'm going to kill myself." People say those words so casually, and it makes me mad. I wonder if these people would say such things if they knew all that suicide involves and how it hurts those people who are left behind.

Now I pay attention if I hear someone threaten suicide or if I see some of the warning signs in people I know. One part of me feels scared that there's nothing I can do, but another part of me says, I have to help. I think I might have a second chance to help someone in a way I never helped Caroline.

Marie, age 25: Caroline and I had a fight that summer. We didn't talk for a while, but finally I called up and said it was pretty silly for us to keep on fighting. We reestablished our friendship and began talking a lot more. Caroline had been going through some rough times—I remember a lot of late-night phone calls when Caroline was falling apart. She had a lot of problems at home. She felt that her father was undermining her self-esteem and that her mother seemed unresponsive to her pleas for help.

Caroline was confused about a lot of things. Although she was dating this guy regularly, she had a lot of doubts about her sexuality. I remember getting her numbers for gay-crisis hot lines so that she could talk to someone who could understand. She told me later that she would talk for hours to some of these people on the phone. While that may have helped at the time, once she was back in her everyday routine she would go through a sort of denial stage and see her boyfriend more than ever.

Caroline needed some counseling to help her deal with everything that was going on in her life. She tried to talk to her mom about everything—to explain the ambiguity she felt over her sexuality and her growing conviction that she was a lesbian. Her mom told her it was just a phase she was going through and brushed it off. Her mom felt there was no need for counseling.

I left for vacation the week before Caroline died. I promised to call her as soon as I came in, but just as I was dialing, I was called away from the phone. I still remember that, I still wonder. . . . By the time I got around to calling Caroline, her father answered her phone. It was her private line, and I remember thinking it was very strange that he should answer, since he never had before. When I asked to speak to Caroline, he told me that she was asleep. I asked him to have her call me when she woke up. . . . I didn't know that she had already died.

Later I was talking to Anne when she got the phone call. I remember her coming back on the line and telling me that she had some bad news—that Caroline had committed suicide. I kept denying it at first—kept asking what hospital she was in. Anne finally got it through to me that Caroline was really dead. Then I flipped out—kicking things, screaming in a rage. I was like that for four days.

Things kept rerunning through my mind—like how some other friends had seen Caroline at a pool party recently, and she had been floating in the pool, looking so peaceful, telling everyone how wonderful life was. The hardest thing to deal with was that Caroline had never said good-bye and hadn't left a note. However, I think she thought very carefully about how she was going to make this attempt. The day she chose was the same date an actor she admired had died in a car crash—she chose that particular day, and a car. I always thought there was some significance to that. But I never really believed that Caroline had meant to die—I still don't.

From what everyone was able to put together, she had asked some friends how long it would take to die from carbon monoxide poisoning, and they had told her several hours. She didn't get into the car until just about an hour before her family was expected home. But her friends had been wrong—with the extreme temperature and humidity, an hour was all it took, and her family was late getting home that day. So what may have started out as a desperate plea for the attention she really needed ended up with her dying.

The wake was unbearably sad. Caroline was buried in her prom dress, and her mom talked to her throughout the day. I remember a lot of people showing up from school—some of whom had heard from friends, others of whom read the obituary in the paper. But no one knew how she had died. That was the hardest part—having to tell Caroline's friends how she died. Her family told people it was an accident at home, so only a few of us really knew. I was shocked when Caroline's boyfriend kept repeating over and over that he couldn't understand how this had happened, asking what kind of accident it was. I remember turning to him, realizing he didn't know. Telling him was very difficult.

The overall memory I have from that time was pain—I remember being in such pain and crying that whole week. I had to be carried out of the funeral. My parents wouldn't let me go to the cemetery, and that bothered me. They felt they were saving me from more pain, but I needed the finality of it, the final good-bye.

For a long time I felt a lot of guilt over Caroline's death, like there was more I could have done. When we returned to school that year, it hit me all over again. I tried to put some pieces together and found out that Caroline had asked a teacher of hers if suicide was a sin. So I had to accept that suicide was something she had been thinking of at the time.

This painting portrays the suicide of Thomas Chatterton, an English poet who died in 1770 at the age of 17. He drank arsenic after a two-month stay in London, when failed attempts to sell his work left him in dire poverty.

After returning to school, I sensed the school officials didn't want to deal with Caroline's death—we were all supposed to pretend it didn't happen. But I just couldn't accept that. I wanted it acknowledged, not hidden because it was a suicide. I tried to put together a memorial service, something we'd done for other students or relatives of students, but was told that it would not be approved. I was put on suicide watch because they felt I couldn't deal with Caroline's death. I was told to get on with my life. They even warned my parents that I could be next. But they never directly spoke to me about what I was feeling.

Looking back, I realize that Caroline's death changed the way I looked at things and altered the future path of my life drastically. Suddenly, going to an Ivy League school didn't seem to matter. Making a lot of money in a profession wasn't important. I really had to rethink my plans and finally decided on psychology. I read as much as I could to understand why people commit suicide and what I could do to help.

I think missing all of Caroline's warning signs made me doubly sure of catching them in someone else in the future. And I did—and was able to prevent the suicide of another classmate as well as help several undergraduates in the dorm I was running while attending grad school.

Religiously, I also changed after Caroline's death. I became involved in a youth group and began to attend retreats. I questioned God, a god who could allow such bad things to happen, but I also came to a better appreciation of my religion and of my friends and family. For

Not every suicide attempt ends in death, and many people who survive go on to lead normal, productive lives. In this rescue scene, onlookers were so concerned about stopping the attempt that some were willing to dive into the freezing Milwaukee River to save the jumper.

several years after Caroline's death I had to hug each friend when we were parting. I never knew when—or if—I'd see them again, and I wanted to show all the people who were important to me that I loved them.

Years later, I've come to terms with any guilt I might have been feeling over Caroline's death. I realize that everyone could have tried to help, but it was ultimately Caroline's decision to take her own life. The words the priest spoke at her funeral stay with me. He said that from that day forward there would always be an empty spot—a void—in our hearts and our lives that Caroline once filled. But that was okay, because that empty spot, all the empty spots, were a living memorial to Caroline and what she meant to each of us.

CHAPTER 7

SURVIVORS OF SUICIDE

Cluster suicides occur when more than one person agrees to commit suicide. Many instances involve lovers, friends, or family members.

I couldn't believe she was actually gone. When we returned to school, I kept looking for her in the crowd of faces, expecting to see her standing by her locker. I had so many questions and no answers. I looked for clues in old pictures, replayed our conversations in my mind, but there was nothing. I still don't understand why she did what she did.

—Lorraine, 17, a friend of Susan's, who committed suicide within the past year

After a suicide has occurred, family members, relatives, and friends remain to cope with their loss and to deal with questions they barely know how to pose, much less answer. Where did I go wrong? What could I have done? How could I not have seen this coming? These questions and many more swirl about in a fog of guilt and despair, leaving the survivors searching to understand the tragedy of suicide.

THE FAMILY

Naturally, family members feel tremendous pain and a sense of loss. Particularly with the suicide of an adolescent, people feel shock and a sense of unfulfilled promise. Parents, especially, feel that their child's death is unnatural—that it goes against the laws of nature for parents to bury their young. It is easy for a parent to feel like a failure and to believe that if he or she had been a successful parent, the suicide would not have occurred.

According to Dr. Thomas Bratter, Cheryl Deep, Dr. Robert C. Kolodny, and Nancy Kolodny, authors of *How to Survive Your Adolescent's Adolescence*, most families of suicide victims in the United States add to their suffering with self-imposed isolation. This makes it harder for the family to accept its loss and begin to put it into perspective.

The authors suggest that the motives behind the isolation are societal. "Suicidologists explain that the reason for such isolation has to do with our culture," they write. "Since the only culturally acceptable

Diane Olton mourns at the funeral of her 18-year-old son, Thomas. He was one of four teenagers involved in a 1987 suicide pact in Bergenfield, New Jersey.

motive for suicide seems to be altruism (for example, fasting to death for a political cause) and since most suicides are not motivated by altruism, the surviving family members receive little or no support from others in coping with their grief."

Parents

Parents often react to the suicide of a child by becoming overly protective of their remaining children. If there are other children living at home, parents may have a heightened fear that these youngsters, too, will kill themselves or die in some other tragic way. This fear, in turn, will often lead parents to smother the surviving children with attention or affection, sometimes questioning and doubting their every move.

Children

Siblings of a suicide victim experience a variety of other emotions. Some may feel anger at their brother's or sister's death—because they could not help, because they have been left behind, or because they feel that the sibling did this to hurt them. Such anger is natural and must be acknowledged, or the surviving children may suffer deepening feelings of guilt and become withdrawn. Siblings of suicide victims may also feel jealousy or resentment after witnessing their parents' grief. They may think, Look how upset Mom and Dad are. Obviously, my brother was more important, and I'm a poor consolation.

During the wake and funeral, and even in the days that follow them, the grieving parents may find it difficult to be there for their other children. Friends, relatives, and the constant stream of condolences may prevent parents from focusing on much else. In addition, the burden of grief and guilt parents bear may leave them in a fog at first. Consequently the surviving children may feel slighted and unimportant and may blame themselves for being unable to comfort their parents.

When a parent has committed suicide, children have very different emotional reactions. Mixed with a sense of guilt is a feeling of blame. The child may blame him- or herself for not having been better or for having been bad. He or she may think, If I wasn't so much trouble, was brighter . . . more popular . . . cleaned my room more often, Mom (or Dad) wouldn't have wanted to die.

Spouses

The spouse of a person who has committed suicide also suffers from tremendous guilt, perhaps replaying in his or her head a litany of shortcomings: If I had cleaned the house more often . . . bought more flowers . . . not gone out as much, he (or she) would still be alive. The surviving mate may suddenly remember every fight, no matter how trivial, that he or she had with a spouse and may come to believe that these arguments led to the suicide. In addition, the partner may externalize these feelings, becoming convinced that others believe that he or she caused the suicide.

The surviving mate of a suicide victim will also have to make tremendous personal and social adjustments. The widow or widower will no longer be part of a couple—a sense of identity that is hard to change under any circumstances. Moreover, old friends may not know how to react to the suicide. Those who are in couples may feel awkward inviting the widowed person to a couples-only setting, such as a dinner party. This awkwardness may lead to a critical loss of support from close friends at a crucial time.

While the remaining mate must struggle to deal with the suicide, and the loss and grief that accompany it, he or she must also face the difficult task of getting the children through that same period. Such people, in need of support themselves, may be unprepared for the daunting task of parenting alone and may be unable to help the children deal with their own confusion. The surviving parent may have extreme difficulty explaining what has happened, particularly when the reasons behind the suicide are unclear. Again, the parent may believe that the children also blame him or her. At these times, other relatives can be an invaluable source of strength and support.

All of these feelings are typical among the family members of a suicide victim. While most feelings pass or decrease over time, some may continue to grow and poison other aspects of that family's life. In

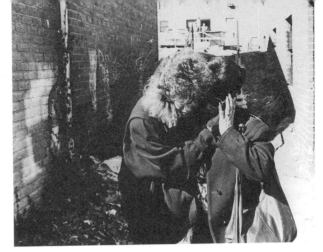

The Bergenfield deaths affected an entire community. An unidentified friend of the four teenagers is overwhelmed with emotion after hearing of the tragedy.

such cases, or at times when a family member simply needs someone objective with whom to talk, counseling or professional help of some sort is recommended.

FRIENDS

Friends of a suicide victim are also susceptible to guilt feelings. They may remember that the troubled person had talked of suicide beforehand but that no one paid serious attention. Regardless of the reasons, friends often feel that they, perhaps even more than the family, should have recognized what was happening and acted to stop it. Having failed to do so, they may hold themselves personally responsible for their friend's death.

If both the victim and the friend are teenagers, additional problems may arise. The suicide may be the first experience that a teen has had with death, and he or she may have difficulty coping or coming to terms with it. Sometimes an adolescent's susceptibility to peer pressure, and the general state of uncertainty many young people feel about the future, may leave the surviving friend open to thoughts of copying the suicide.

CLUSTER AND COPYCAT SUICIDES

On March 11, 1987, at about 3:00 A.M., four teenagers from the quiet New Jersey suburb of Bergenfield bought three dollars' worth of gas from a local gas station and, after being denied permission to take the station's vacuum cleaner hose, drove to a nearby vacant garage. There two girls and two boys rolled down the windows of their Camaro and took turns writing suicide notes on a brown paper bag. They left the car running, and within an hour all four teens were dead. A short time later, a man on his way to work heard the sound of the car engine from the garage and reported it to the police, who discovered the bodies.

The impact of these suicides stunned not only the middle-class community of Bergenfield but the entire nation as well. Media representatives poured into the small town and vied for spots in front of the high school that all four teenagers had attended. Microphones were thrust at neighbors, classmates, and friends as television stations fought for material for the evening's news programs. Lurid headlines screamed of the teen death pact, rehashing stories of other such pacts in previous years.

The tragedy at the Peoples' Temple at Jonestown, in the South American country of Guyana, involved one of the largest group suicides in history. On November 18, 1978, American cult leader Jim Jones induced more than 900 of his followers, including parents and their children, to die together by drinking a cyanide-laced fruit punch.

At the same time, the Bergenfield community attempted to deal with the tragic blow. School officials held assemblies and added extra counseling to the daily schedule. Local programs to help teens were publicized, encouraging troubled adolescents to make full use of them. Parents, panicking over the effect the suicides might have on their own children, held on to their youngsters a little tighter. All the while, the people of Bergenfield, along with the rest of the nation, tried to understand what had happened and why.

Although the suicide pact in itself was shocking, it was easier to see how such a thing might have happened once all of the facts were known. The victims were Cheryl Burress, 17; her 16-year-old sister, Lisa; Thomas Olton, 18; and Thomas Rizzo, 19. Among them were histories of problems with school, substance abuse, previous suicide attempts, and ongoing family trouble. In addition, there had been four other suspicious Bergenfield deaths in the previous nine months that investigators felt may have been suicides—and at least one of those may have provided an impetus in this particular case.

The death of Joe Major, a friend of all four of the dead teens, just six months earlier could have given them the idea. Major had fallen to his death 200 feet below the Palisades, a series of cliffs overlooking the Hudson River. Although the death was ruled accidental—the result of too much drinking—some classmates felt that Major's death had actually been suicide. Lisa Burress had dated Major and had not yet accepted his death. Both she and Rizzo had been there when he fell.

Aside from their links with Major's death, all four teens had experienced trouble in school. Rizzo, Olton, and Cheryl Burress were all high school dropouts, and Lisa Burress had just been suspended. Rumors suggested that Olton's father had committed suicide. In addition, both boys had at one time been treated for substance abuse problems, and the Burress sisters were struggling to cope with their mother's remarriage.

In the suicide notes, the four had requested a joint wake and burial. Their parents, however, refused to honor the request, perhaps feeling that to do so would have been to glamorize the deaths. Many teenagers do think of suicide as glamorous, which helps explain the allure it holds for so many. Pamela Cantor, president of the National Committee for the Prevention of Youth Suicide, addressed this in the March 23, 1987, issue of *Time* magazine: "Kids perceive this as a glamorous way to die, a way to get attention that they couldn't get in life." She added, "They see a kid that is a nonentity suddenly get attention, which is what they have been struggling for."

If, after seeing the attention another person's suicide receives, an individual takes his or her own life, the act is known as a *copycat suicide*. Cluster suicides and copycat suicides occur primarily among teenagers.

Less than two days after the Bergenfield suicides, an apparent copycat suicide pact was discovered in Alsip, Illinois, a suburb of Chicago. Two young women, Nancy Grannan, 19, and her friend Karen Logan, 17, were found in the carbon monoxide–filled garage of the Logan family home. Several suicide notes were found as well.

The young women had been close friends. Both were high school dropouts and unemployed. Grannan's marriage had recently failed, and she was still depressed over two miscarriages. For several days prior to their death, both women had been drinking heavily. Although both victims had probably considered suicide before, investigators felt that media coverage of the Bergenfield deaths may have influenced their decision.

Even though the Bergenfield suicides had followed other questionable deaths, they would not be considered copycats. Instead, they would be classified as a *cluster*. In a study reported in the November 17, 1989, issue of the *Journal of the American Medical Association*, Dr. Lucy Davidson and associates defined cluster suicides as "three or more suicides that occur within a defined space and time."

The study of cluster suicides can provide researchers with useful clues as to what drives an adolescent to take his or her own life and what conditions are common to a majority of teen suicide cases. In this way, researchers may be able to predict who is most likely to attempt suicide and what social factors may have contributed to this tendency. If researchers can determine who might be more susceptible to suicide, they can develop a composite personality type or a list of criteria. Then school personnel, counselors, and parents may be able to foresee

A well-known instance of cluster suicides occurred in the suburban community of League City, Texas (bordering the Houston metropolitan area), in 1984. This special panel of psychologists investigated the cause of six teenage suicides that occurred over a ten-week period.

suicidal tendencies in a particular child and get him or her the necessary care and attention.

To that end, Davidson and her associates conducted a study of two teen suicide clusters that occurred in Texas between February 1983 and October 1984. Researchers compared data collected from the families of the 8 suicides in the first cluster and the 6 in the second with a control group of 42 teenagers.

The researchers were able to draw a number of conclusions regarding possible risk factors in teen cluster suicides. The study reported that the adolescents who committed suicide "were more likely to have attempted or threatened suicide previously, to have damaged themselves physically, and to have known someone closely who died violently." In addition, they were "more likely to have broken up with their girlfriends or boyfriends recently . . . [and] had moved more often than control subjects, attended more schools, and lived with more parent figures."

The potential to use the conclusions drawn from this and similar studies is tremendous. The study concludes, "Identification of high-risk youths through knowledge of relevant risk factors can help to direct preventive services to those young people most susceptible to suicide." With more services and individual counseling available to troubled teenagers before they attempt to take their own life, there is a greater chance of effectively combating the growing teen suicide rate in the United States.

CHAPTER 8

TREATMENT AND PREVENTION

In response to six cluster suicides in Plano, Texas, in 1983, high school counselors organized group sessions to discuss the topic of suicide openly.

Once a suicide has been attempted, professional help should be sought. Aside from the physical damage that may have resulted from the attempt, the underlying emotional reasons must be examined and dealt with. A counselor, psychiatrist, or psychologist may be best able to help the individual and his or her family and friends.

Hospitalization may be necessary, however, if there is a risk of a repeat attempt. This usually involves confinement in the psychiatric ward of a hospital and placing the patient on suicide watch. The individual is observed for any future attempts to take his or her life and is allowed no opportunities to do so. Such patients are either put under constant surveillance or kept away from any object that could be used for self-destruction. A shaving razor or a bed sheet can become dangerous objects in the hands of a suicidal individual.

While some people are reluctant to undergo hospitalization, it does offer a number of benefits. A period of hospitalization gives the patient time to reflect on the seriousness of his or her actions instead of allowing the individual to brush it off. Additionally, the person receives care 24 hours a day, and someone is always ready to listen, something the patient may have lacked before attempting suicide in the first place.

Even without hospitalization, an individual who has attempted to take his or her own life will need some psychological guidance. Because many of the problems that led to the attempt may stem from family life, the family members—spouse, siblings, or parents—are

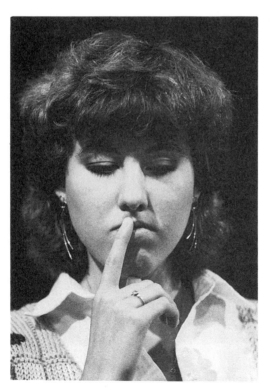

This 16-year-old prefers to remain anonymous. After attempting suicide three times, she testified before a Senate Judiciary Juvenile Justice Subcommittee that "no matter how bad things may seem, they will get better."

often asked to attend group therapy sessions. These sessions allow free expression of thoughts and feelings and enable the therapist to observe family dynamics.

Finding the appropriate type of mental health treatment is also important. The method of therapy required can be assessed only on a case-by-case basis. From the different treatment options available, the individual, the family, and the physician must decide what would be best. If a substance abuse problem is involved, proper treatment must also be sought for that.

Treatment options available for substance abusers include hospitalization and 12-step treatment programs such as Alcoholics Anonymous (AA) and Narcotics Anonymous (NA). Both AA and NA have decades of proven experience behind them. In addition, programs such as Al-Anon and Nar-Anon offer similar support for spouses and family members of substance abusers. There are also a number of alcohol and drug rehabilitation centers nationwide, each with its own treatment option. A physician or the local department of health or human services can recommend specific programs.

Monica Dickens, founder of an international suicide prevention group called the Samaritans, points to the 12-foot-high steel rods installed to prevent further suicides occurring from the Bourne Bridge in Massachusetts. She is pictured with Frank Ciccone, who oversaw construction of the barrier by the U.S. Army Corps of Engineers in 1981.

STAR CENTER—Services for Teens at Risk

Many people who work with suicide prevention feel that not enough has been done to help teenagers who call in with problems. They feel that teens consider suicide when they feel unable to cope with their problems. In recent years, experienced counselors have searched for methods to help teens approach and solve their problems.

One well-regarded expert is Dr. David Brent, a psychiatrist known for his work with teen suicide. In 1986, he founded the STAR (Services for Teens at Risk) Center, a facility that has gained national recognition for its work. The program is innovative because it concentrates specifically on suicidal teenagers.

The center defines three steps necessary for successful suicide intervention: early recognition of the problem, appropriate referral for treatment, and continuing research into the causes of suicide. The center puts these steps into effect with an outreach program, an outpatient clinic, and an extensive research program.

The outreach program teaches training and intervention techniques in local school systems. It instructs administrators, teachers, and social workers—those professionals in daily contact with young people—to identify suicide risk factors and learn referral procedures. The program goes a step further, however, by training these people to evaluate a young person's level of risk and then to work with the student and his or her family to resolve misunderstandings and encourage communication. Finally, the outreach program also instructs trainees on methods of educating other personnel within their organizations.

In addition, the center offers outpatient treatment through the Western Psychiatric Institute and Clinic, at the University of Pittsburgh. Typically, a plan of treatment includes a complete psychiatric assessment, then individually based *cognitive therapy* and *behavior therapy* that emphasize communication and problem-solving skills. (Cognitive therapy helps clients overcome distortions in their thinking; behavior therapy teaches clients ways to change disruptive habits.) This program also enables researchers to evaluate various methods of therapy for young people in order to improve future methods of treatment.

In early discussions with a

client, the interviewer or counselor will make a brief assessment of the following symptoms:

- Depression.
- Extreme depression—moody, slowed down (if this applies, the individual is probably in dire need of help).
- Alcohol or drug abuse.
- Behavior problems at school.
- Divorce or abuse at home.

When the clinic first undertakes work with a troubled individual, the initial five hours are used for evaluation, usually taking one hour per day. During this time, an entire interview is devoted to assessing depression. Parents of troubled teenagers are also interviewed, and the importance of parental involvement in treatment is stressed.

Although the program does not include a hot-line center, experts at the clinic can respond to emergency calls from young people contemplating suicide or from concerned guidance counselors, pediatricians, or parents. When a teenager or concerned loved one first contacts the center, the interviewer tries to obtain preliminary information concerning the client's demographics (such as age, address, and school), the purpose behind the call, and the amount of danger the person is in.

Factors that indicate a caller is seriously considering suicide include the following:

- Previous suicidal behavior, particularly attempts that have come close to succeeding.
- Present state of mind and thoughts of suicide.
- Current suicide plan.
- Weapons present in the home (because most suicides are caused by gunshot).
- Strong feelings of hopelessness.

Hopelessness is considered the most serious danger sign, and a client's attitudes about the future often indicate his or her level of hopelessness. An interviewer gains insight by asking whether the client is looking forward to anything, what the client sees him- or herself doing in a couple of weeks, and if he or she has told anyone about a suicide plan. (Most suicidal people let someone know before taking action.)

Before the center agrees to see an individual at risk, the interviewer asks the caller to hold to a verbal "no suicide contract" in which the client agrees not to hurt him- or herself before the initial interview. The contract also asks the caller to visit an emergency room if he or she feels out of control or to confide his or her feelings to someone trustworthy. Then the interviewer will try to arrange an appointment so that the individual at risk can meet with a counselor within seven days.

PREVENTION

Naturally, the best way to handle a suicide attempt is to prevent it from occurring in the first place. Although many people believe that once someone has made up his or her mind to commit suicide very little can be done to stop the attempt, the reverse is actually true. The following list of suggestions may help to prevent a tragedy.

- If a friend or relative seems very depressed or talks frequently of suicide, encourage that individual to see a professional therapist or counselor. Seeking such help will not mean the person is "crazy" but indicates that he or she needs someone who will listen and provide guidance through this rough spot in life. It may help to remind the individual that everyone at some point suffers from problems that are too difficult to work through alone and that there is no shame in admitting it.

- If the person refuses to see a mental health professional, suggest that he or she speak to a physician, clergy member, teacher, or guidance counselor. All of these people are trained to counsel troubled individuals and may even be able to convince such a person to see a therapist.

- In the case of an adolescent who may be considering suicide, inform the teen's guidance counselor or a favorite teacher, as well as his or her parents, of the danger. Although this may anger the youth, saving his or her life must take precedence. Parents often fail to realize that their child is considering suicide. Letting them know gives them the opportunity to show how much they care and to support their youngster through a rough time. Sadly, many parents find out just how disturbed their child was only after it is too late to help.

- Encourage the person to call a suicide-prevention or crisis-intervention hot line such as the ones listed in the back of this book. The hot lines are staffed by trained personnel who offer guidance to troubled individuals—often around the clock.

- Confront a friend who appears troubled and may be considering suicide. He or she may be hoping for the opportunity to open up and discuss a problem. In any case, talking will demonstrate to the individual that

Experts agree that communication offers the best chance for suicide prevention. Family members who are willing to discuss their difficulties, no matter how deep the problems may be, are much more likely to overcome feelings of isolation, hopelessness, and despair.

someone cares enough to be interested in his or her welfare. By the same token, if a friend confides that he or she has planned a suicide attempt, do not keep the secret.

- If an individual who has been very depressed suddenly and unexpectedly adopts the attitude that everything is fine, there may be cause for concern. He or she may have resolved to commit suicide and feel relieved over having made the decision. Seek help immediately.

- Most importantly, listen. Listen to what people are saying—or not saying. Parents should listen to their children for any signs of depression. Teens should listen to their friends for any sign of suicidal thoughts. Teachers and school administrators should listen to their students and be aware of the types of questions these young people are asking.

If more people listened to and actually heard each other, there would be fewer breakdowns in communication, fewer people feeling lonely and uncared for, and, consequently, fewer suicides.

"All he needs is a good swift kick in the pants."

How many times have we thought this about a loved one who isn't performing up to our expectations.

We see their depression as a bad attitude. Misread their self-centeredness as a personality problem. Believe their inability to cope with daily activities is laziness.

But sometimes inappropriate behavior may be a warning sign of something more serious. A mental illness.

Mental illness is a medical illness—not a personal weakness. And learning to recognize its warning signs can be the first step to healing the sickness.

Learn more. For an informative booklet, write: The American Mental Health Fund, P.O. Box 17700, Washington, D.C. 20041. Or call toll free: 1-800-433-5959. In Illinois, call: 1-800-826-2336.

Learn to see the sickness. Learning is the key to healing.

THE AMERICAN MENTAL HEALTH FUND

APPENDIX I:
FOR MORE INFORMATION

The following is a list of organizations in the United States and Canada that can provide more information on suicide and related topics.

GENERAL INFORMATION

American Association of Suicidology
Central Office
2459 South Ash
Denver, CO 80222
(303) 692-0985

International Association for Suicide
    Prevention
c/o Charlotte P. Ross
Suicide Prevention of San Mateo
    County
1811 Trousdale Drive
Burlingame, CA 94010
(415) 692-6662

Samaritans
500 Commonwealth Avenue
Boston, MA 02215
(617) 247-0220

Youth Suicide National Center
204 East 2nd Avenue, Suite 203
San Mateo, CA 94401
(415) 347-3961

AIDS AND TERMINAL ILLNESS

AIDS Action Council
Federation of AIDS-Related Organizations
2033 M Street NW, Suite 802
Washington, DC 20036
(202) 293-2886

AIDS Network of Edmonton
10704 108th Street
Edmonton, Alberta T5H 3A3
Canada
(403) 424-4767

American Red Cross
AIDS Education Office
431 18th Street NW
Washington, DC 20006
(202) 737-8300

Canadian AIDS Society
170 Laurier Avenue West, Suite 1801
Ottawa, Ontario K1P 5Z5
Canada
(613) 230-3580

Gay Men's Health Crisis (GMHC)
132 West 24th Street, Box 274
New York, NY 10011
(212) 807-6655

Minority Task Force on AIDS
c/o New York City Council of Churches
92 Nicholas Avenue, Suite 1B
New York, NY 10026
(212) 749-2816

National AIDS Hotline
1-800-342-AIDS

National AIDS Network
729 Eighth Street, Suite 300
Washington, DC 20003
(202) 483-7979

National Gay and Lesbian Task Force
    Hotline
80 Fifth Avenue, Suite 1601
New York, NY 10011
(800) 221-7044

People with AIDS
31 West 26th Street
New York, NY 10010
(212) 532-0568

ALCOHOLISM

Al-Anon Family Group Headquarters
1372 Broadway
New York, NY 10018
(212) 302-7240

Al-Anon Family Groups
Canada
(613) 722-1830
(613) 725-3431
(referrals for counseling)

Alcohol and Drug Problems Association
    of America (ADPA)
1400 Eye Street NW, Suite 1275

Washington, DC 20005
(202) 289-6755

Alcoholics Anonymous
P.O. Box 459
15 East 26th Street
New York, NY 10010
(212) 683-3900

Alcoholics Anonymous
234 Eglinton Avenue East, Suite 502
Toronto, Ontario M4P 1K5
Canada
(416) 487-5591

Hazelden Foundation
P.O. Box 11
Center City, MN 55012
(800) 262-5010, Ext. 3307

DEPRESSION

American Mental Health Foundation
2 East 86th Street
New York, NY 10028
(212) 737-9027

Canadian Mental Health Association
Metro Toronto Branch
970 Lawrence Avenue West, Suite 205
Toronto, Ontario M6A 3B6
Canada
(416) 789-7957

National Depressive and Manic Depres-
    sive Association
P.O. Box 3395
Chicago, IL 60654
(312) 993-0066

National Institute of Mental Health
Alcohol, Drug Abuse, and Mental
    Health Administration
5600 Fishers Lane
Room 12-105
Rockville, MD 20857

(301) 443-4797
(Administrator's office)

DRUG ABUSE

Help Line
12280 Wilkins Avenue
Rockville, MD 20852
(800) 662-HELP

Canadian Centre on Substance Abuse
112 Kent Street
Place de Ville Tower B, Suite 480
Ottawa, Ontario K1P 5P2
Canada
(613) 235-4048

Cocaine Anonymous
P.O. Box 2058
Canal Steet Station
New York, NY 10013
(212) 262-2463
(referrals for treatment)

Drugs Anonymous
P.O. Box 173
Ansonia Station
New York, NY 10023
(212) 874-0700

1-800-COCAINE
P.O. Box 100
Summit, NJ 07902-0100
(referrals for treatment; parents must
    call for minors)

Phoenix House Foundation
164 West 74th Street
New York, NY 10023
(212) 595-5810

Rubicon, Inc.
1300 MacTavish Avenue
Richmond, VA 23230
(804) 359-3255

Straight, Inc.
3001 Gandy Blvd.
St. Petersburg, FL 33702
(813) 576-8929

Target: Helping Students Cope with Al-
    cohol and Drugs
P.O. Box 20626
11724 Plaza Circle
Kansas City, MO 64195
(800) 366-6667
(referrals for treatment)

EUTHANASIA

Concern for Dying (Euthanasia)
250 West 57th Street
New York, NY 10107
(212) 246-6962

Dying with Dignity
Canadian Society Concerned with the
    Quality of Dying
175 St. Clair Avenue West
Toronto, Ontario M4V 1P7
Canada
(416) 921-2329

Hemlock Society
P.O. Box 11830
Eugene, OR 97440-3900
(503) 342-5748

Society for the Right to Die
250 West 57th Street
New York, NY 10107
(212) 246-6973

MENTAL ILLNESS

American Association of Psychiatric
    Services for Children
3615 Wisconsin Avenue NW
Washington, DC 20016
(202) 966-7300

Friends of Schizophrenics
c/o Canadian Mental Health Association
  (CMHA)
1355 Bank Street, Suite 402
Ottawa, Ontario K1H 8K7
Canada
(613) 737-7636

National Alliance for the Mentally Ill
2101 Wilson Blvd.
Suite 302
Arlington, VA 22201

STATE LISTINGS

The following is a list of suicide and crisis hot lines throughout the United States and Canada. Any number listed as a business phone can be called to obtain information about that organization.

ALABAMA

Crisis Center of Jefferson County
3600 Eighth Avenue South
Birmingham, AL 35222
(205) 323-7777
(205) 223-7782
(business phone)

ALASKA

South Central Counseling
4020 Folkner
Anchorage, AK 99508
(907) 276-1600

ARIZONA

Camelback Hospital
5055 North 34th Street
Phoenix, AZ 85018
(800) 274-2995

Stress Line
1424 South Seventh Avenue
Phoenix, AZ 85007
(602) 271-0695

ARKANSAS

Arkansas Crisis Suicide Center
1623 North Main Street
North Little Rock, AR 72114
(501) 372-1122

CALIFORNIA

Los Angeles Suicide Prevention Center
1041 South Menlos
Los Angeles, CA 90006
(213) 381-5111
(213) 385-3752
(business phone)

San Francisco Suicide Prevention
3940 Geary Blvd.
San Francisco, CA 94118
(415) 221-1423
(415) 752-4866
(business phone)

COLORADO

Suicide and Crisis Control
2459 South Ash Street
Denver, CO 80222
(303) 756-8485
(303) 757-0988
(303) 789-3073

Suicide Depression Crisis Hotline
(303) 860-1200

CONNECTICUT

Contact
P.O. Box 249

West Mystic, CT 06388
(203) 848-1281

DELAWARE

Mental Health Association in Delaware
1813 N. Franklin Street
Wilmington, DE 19803
(302) 656-8300
(800) 287-MHAD
(in Delaware; outside the Wilmington area)

DISTRICT OF COLUMBIA

Samaritan Suicide Hotline
(202) 362-8100

FLORIDA

University of Miami Medical Center
Box 016960
Miami, FL 33101
(305) 674-2194

GEORGIA

Emergency Mental Health Service
99 Butler Street
Atlanta, GA 30303
(404) 730-1600

HAWAII

Suicide and Crisis Center
200 N. Vineyard Blvd.
Honolulu, HI 96817
(808) 521-4555
(808) 536-7234
(business phone)

IDAHO

Suicide Hotline
Mercy Medical Center

1512 12th Avenue Road
Nampa, ID 83651
(208) 465-2121

ILLINOIS

Contact Chicago
401 East Illinois, #324
Chicago, IL 60611
(312) 644-4357
(312) 644-4900
(business phone)

Rush Medical College
9400 Lebanon Road
Edgemont, IL 62203
(312) 942-5372

INDIANA

Mental Health Association
Marion County
1433 North Meridian Street, Suite 202
Indianapolis, IN 46202-2395
(317) 632-7575

IOWA

AID Center
206 6th Street
Sioux City, IA 51101
(712) 252-5000
(712) 252-1861

KANSAS

Johnson County Mental Health Center
6000 Lamar Street, Suite 130
Mission, KS 66202
(913) 384-3535

KENTUCKY

Comprehensive Care
201 Mechanic Street

Lexington, KY 40507
(606) 233-0444

LOUISIANA

Baton Rouge Crisis Intervention Center
P.O. Box 80738
Baton Rouge, LA 70898
(504) 924-3900
(504) 928-6482
(business phone)

MAINE

Ingraham Volunteers
74 Elm Street
Portland, ME 04101
(207) 774-HELP

MARYLAND

Montgomery County Crisis Center
4910 Auburn Avenue
Bethesda, MD 20814
(301) 656-9420

MASSACHUSETTS

The Samaritans
500 Commonwealth Avenue
Boston, MA 02215
(617) 247-0220
(617) 536-2460
(business phone)

MICHIGAN

Suicide Prevention Center
220 Bagley, Suite 626
Detroit, MI 48226
(313) 224-7000
(313) 963-7890
(business phone)

MINNESOTA

Lovelines, Inc.
2701 4th Street South East
Minneapolis, MN 55414
(612) 379-1199

MISSISSIPPI

Contact
P.O. Box 5192
Jackson, MS 39296-1592
(601) 982-1221

MISSOURI

Western Missouri Mental Health Center
600 East 22nd Street
Kansas City, MO 64108
(816) 471-3939

MONTANA

Mental Health Center
1245 N. 29th Street
Billings, MT 59101
(406) 252-5658
(406) 252-1212
(after hours)

NEBRASKA

Personal Crisis Center
(402) 475-5171

NEVADA

Suicide Prevention and Crisis Call
  Center
P.O. Box 8016
Reno, NV 89507
(702) 323-6111
(800) 992-5757
(in Nevada; outside the Reno area)

NEW HAMPSHIRE

Riverbend Counseling Center
P.O. Box 2032
Concord, NH 03302
(603) 228-0547

NEW JERSEY

Psychiatric Intervention Program
1925 Pacific Avenue
Atlantic City, NJ 08401
(609) 344-1118

NEW MEXICO

Agora
The University of New Mexico Crisis
    Center
Student Union
P.O. Box 29
Albuquerque, NM 87131
(505) 277-3013
(505) 277-7855
(business phone)

NEW YORK

The Samaritans of New York City
P.O. Box 1259
Madison Square Station
New York, NY 10159
(212) 673-3000
(provides suicide hot lines as well as counseling services for those who have lost a loved one through suicide)

NORTH CAROLINA

The Relatives, Inc.
1100 E. Boulevard
Charlotte, NC 28203
(704) 377-0602
(707) 335-0203
(business phone)

NORTH DAKOTA

Hotline
P.O. Box 447
Fargo, ND 58107
(701) 232-4357

OHIO

Crisis Hotline
513 West Market Street
Akron, OH 44303
(216) 434-9144

OKLAHOMA

Tulsa Helpline
P.O. Box 52847
Tulsa, OK 74152
(918) 583-4357
(918) 585-1144
(business phone)

OREGON

White Bird Clinic
341 E. 12th Avenue
Eugene, OR 97401
(503) 342-8255
(503) 687-4000

PENNSYLVANIA

Contact Pittsburgh, Inc.
P.O. Box 111294
Pittsburgh, PA 15238
(412) 782-4023

Services for Teens at Risk (STAR
    Center)
Western Psychiatric Institute and Clinic
3811 O'Hara Street
Pittsburgh, PA 15213
(412) 624-1000

RHODE ISLAND

The Samaritans of Rhode Island
2 Magee Street
Providence, RI 02906
(401) 272-4044

SOUTH CAROLINA

Helpline of the Midlands, Inc.
P.O. Box 6336
Columbia, SC 29260
(803) 790-4357
(803) 782-3771
(business phone)

SOUTH DAKOTA

Crisis Line, Volunteer, and Information
   Center
304 S. Phillips Avenue
Sioux Falls, SD 51702
(605) 339-4357
(605) 334-7022

TENNESSEE

Crisis Center
P.O. Box 40752
Nashville, TN 37201-0752
(615) 244-7444

TEXAS

Crisis Intervention of Houston, Inc.
P.O. Box 130866
Houston, TX 77219
(713) 228-1505

Suicide and Crisis Center
2808 Swiss Avenue
Dallas, TX 75204
(214) 828-1000
(214) 824-7020
(business phone)

UTAH

Salt Lake Valley Mental Health
1228 S. 900 E
Salt Lake City, UT 84105
(801) 483-5444

VERMONT

Orange County Mental Health Service
Emergency Service
P.O. Box G
Randolph, VT 05060
(800) 639-6360
(802) 728-4466
(business phone)

VIRGINIA

Northern Virginia Hotline
P.O. Box 187
Arlington, VA 22210
(703) 527-4077

WASHINGTON

Crisis Clinic
1530 Eastlake East
Seattle, WA 98102
(206) 461-3222

WEST VIRGINIA

Upper Ohio Valley Crisis Hotline
P.O. Box 653
Wheeling, WV 26003
(304) 234-8161
(304) 234-1848
(business phone)

WISCONSIN

Crisis Intervention Center
131 S. Madison Street

Green Bay, WI 54301
(414) 432-8832

WYOMING

Cheyenne Helpline
P.O. Box 404
Cheyenne, WY 82003
(307) 634-4469
(307) 632-4132
(business phone)

CANADA

Distress Center of Ottawa
(613) 238-3311

Military Family Support Center
F.M.O. Halifax
2730 Gottigen Street
Halifax, Nova Scotia B3K 2X0
(902) 427-8100

Tel-Aide Montreal
C.P. 205, Succursale 'H'
Montreal, Quebec H3G 2K7
(514) 935-1101
(514) 935-1105
(business phone)

Toronto East General Hospital
Department of Psychiatry
825 Coxwell Avenue
Toronto, Ontario M4C 3E7
(416) 461-0311

APPENDIX II:
RISK FACTORS

The following is a list of factors that may increase a person's risk of suicide.

- A history of alcohol or substance abuse

- Financial pressures, such as the loss of a job

- The loss of a loved one

- The loss of a friend or family member to suicide

- A stressful family life

- A serious, debilitating, or fatal illness

- Employment in certain high-stress professions, including in the medical and legal fields and law enforcement

- Respiratory difficulty at birth

- The pressure of overly high expectations to excel

- Problems with school or the law

- Increased competition created by a larger peer group

- The breakup of a romance

- An unplanned pregnancy

- A family history of suicide

- Having parents who are depressed or are substance abusers

- A loss of security or confidence due to new situations, such as beginning college or relocating to a new community

APPENDIX III:
SOME WARNING SIGNS
OF SUICIDAL BEHAVIOR

The following list may offer clues to an impending suicide attempt.

- Recent disinterest in normal activities and in life in general

- Deep depression followed by a "high." Individual seems resolved and happy for the first time in a long time; seems to have reached a decision

- Giving away belongings

- Saying good-bye and tying up loose ends

- Having trouble at home, in school, or on the job

- A preoccupation with death, dying, or suicide

- Talking or joking about death or suicide

- Alcohol or substance abuse

- The recent death of a close friend or relative, especially if by suicide

- Change in eating and sleeping habits, such as insomnia or anorexia

- Poor grooming habits

- Poor grades

- An indifferent attitude toward potentially dangerous situations

- A previous suicide attempt

FURTHER READING

GENERAL INFORMATION

Baker, Sherry. "Born Under a Bad Sign." *Omni* 11 (November 1988).

"Bergenfield's Tragic Foursome." *U.S. News and World Report* 102 (March 23, 1987): 11.

Cutter, Fred. *Art and the Wish to Die*. Chicago: Nelson-Hall, 1983.

Davidson, Lucy E., Mark L. Rosenberg, James A. Mercy, Jack Franklin, and Jane T. Simmons. "An Epidemiologic Study of Risk Factors in Two Teenage Suicide Clusters." *Journal of the American Medical Association* 262 (November 1989).

Eckman, Fern Marja. "Teen Suicide." *McCall's* 115 (October 1987).

Folkenberg, Judy. "Suicide Chemistry: Low Growth Hormone May Signal Suicide Risk." *American Health* 8 (May 1989): 107.

Giovacchini, Peter. *The Urge to Die*. New York: Penguin Books, 1981.

Hafen, Brent Q., and Kathryn J. Frandsen. *Youth Suicide*. Evergreen, CO: Cordillera Press, 1986.

Hoagland, Edward. "The Urge for an End: Contemplating Suicide." *Harper's* 276 (March 1988): 45.

Keir, Norman. *I Can't Face Tomorrow*. Rochester, VT: Thorsons, 1986.

Kennedy, Thomas D. "Suicide and the Silence of the Scripture." *Christianity Today* 31 (March 1987): 22.

Kolodny, Robert C., Nancy J. Kolodny, Thomas Bratter, and Cheryl Deep. *How to Survive Your Adolescent's Adolescence*. Boston: Little, Brown, 1984.

Madison, Arnold. *Suicide and Young People*. New York: Clarion, 1978.

Maris, Ronald W. *Pathways to Suicide*. Baltimore: Johns Hopkins University Press, 1981.

Martz, Larry. "Copycat Suicides: Two Death Pacts Kill Six Troubled Teenagers, Triggering Fears of a New National Epidemic." *Newsweek* 109 (March 23, 1987): 28.

Mohler, Mary. "Teen Suicide: The Sobering Facts." *Ladies Home Journal* 104 (November 1987): 106.

Wilentz, Amy. "Teen Suicide: Two Death Pacts Shake the Country." *Time* 129 (March 1987): 12.

Witkin, Gordon. "Groping to Cope with Teen Suicides: Communities Respond." *U.S. News and World Report* 102 (March 30, 1987): 12.

AIDS AND TERMINAL ILLNESS

Caughill, Rita E. *The Dying Patient: A Supportive Approach*. Boston: Little, Brown, 1976.

Marzuk, Peter M., Helen Tierney, Kenneth Tardiff, Elliot Gross, and Edward B. Morgan. "Increased Risk of Suicide in Persons with AIDS." *Journal of the American Medical Association* 259 (March 1988): 1333.

Slaby, Andrew E., and Arvin S. Glicksman. *Adapting to Life Threatening Illness*. New York: Praeger, 1985.

ALCOHOLISM AND DRUG ABUSE

Bower, Bruce. "Drug Abuse Tied to 'Fatal Despondency.'" *Science News* 135 (May 1989).

———. "Drugs and Suicide: Link to Recent Loss." *Science News* 133 (June 1988).

Gold. *Facts About Drugs and Alcohol*. New York: Bantam Books, 1987.

Goodwin, Donald W. *Alcoholism: The Facts*. New York: Oxford University Press, 1981.

Hazelden. *Learn About Youth and Drug Addiction*. Center City, MN: Hazelden, 1985.

Johnson, Vernon E. *Intervention: How to Help Someone Who Doesn't Want Help*. New York: New American Library, 1988.

Mumey, Jack. *Young Alcoholics: A Book for Parents*. Chicago, IL: Contemporary Books, 1986.

Ryan, Elizabeth A. *Straight Talk About Drugs and Alcohol*. New York: Facts on File, 1988.

DEATH AND DYING

Kübler-Ross, Elisabeth. *Living with Death and Dying*. New York: Collier, 1981.

Ogg, Elisabeth. *Facing Death and Loss*. Lancaster, PA: Technomic, 1985.

Schultz, Richard. *The Psychology of Death, Dying, and Bereavement.* Reading, MA: Addison-Wesley, 1978.

Whaley, Joachim, ed. *Mirrors of Mortality: Studies in the Social History of Death.* New York: St. Martin's Press, 1981.

DEPRESSION

Andersen, N. C. *The Broken Brain: The Biological Revolution in Psychiatry.* New York: HarperCollins, 1984.

Costello, Charles Gerard. *Anxiety and Depression: The Adaptive Emotions.* Montreal: McGill–Queens University Press, 1976.

Good, Byron, and Arthur Kleinman, eds. *Culture and Depression: Studies in the Anthropology and Cross-Cultural Psychiatry of Affect and Disorder.* Berkeley: University of California Press, 1985.

Griest, John H., and James W. Jefferson. *Depression and Its Treatment.* New York: American Psychiatrist/Warner Books, 1984.

EUTHANASIA

Campbell, Robert, and Diane Collinson. *Ending Lives.* New York: Basil Blackwell, N. d.

Humphrey, Derek, and Ann Wickett. *The Right to Die: Understanding Euthanasia.* New York: HarperCollins, 1987.

Rachels, James. *The End of Life: Euthanasia and Mortality.* New York: Oxford University Press, 1986.

Wallace, Samuel E., and Abin Eser, eds. *Suicide and Euthanasia.* Knoxville: University of Tennessee, 1981.

GLOSSARY

AIDS acquired immune deficiency syndrome; an acquired defect in the immune system; the final stage of the disease caused by the human immunodeficiency virus (HIV); leaves victims vulnerable to infections and cancers that are often fatal

alcoholism the excessive use of alcoholic beverages causing deterioration in health and social relations; characterized by physical dependency on alcohol and damage to the liver, the brain, and the nervous and digestive systems

amphetamines any of a number of drugs that stimulate parts of the central nervous system

barbiturates any of the various drugs that cause depression of the nervous system

breech birth delivery of a fetus with the hind end of its body appearing first

carbon monoxide poisoning suffocation due to the respiration of carbon monoxide, a colorless, odorless toxic gas

cesarean section surgical incision of the abdomen and uterus to deliver a baby

chloroform a colorless toxic liquid used as a solvent or general anesthetic

cluster suicides suicides that take place in a specific geographic area over a short period of time; sometimes the result of a suicide pact

cocaine psychosis an illness associated with chronic use of cocaine and characterized by hallucinations and loss of touch with reality

control group a group used as a standard of comparison for the experimental effects on other groups in a scientific study

copycat suicides suicides occurring soon after other suicides; committed by people who have known or heard about someone who committed suicide

Council of Braga a Roman Catholic council of bishops that officially declared suicide a sin; met in Braga, Portugal, in A.D. 563

depressant a drug or other agent that reduces the activity of bodily functions

depression when used to describe a mood, includes feelings of sadness, despair, and discouragement; when used to describe a disorder, refers to a syndrome of associated symptoms, including decreased pleasure, slowed thinking, sadness, hopelessness, guilt, and disrupted sleeping and eating patterns

detoxification the process whereby a person is freed of his or her dependence on an addictive drug; also, the removal of any poison or toxin from the body

epidemiologist a specialist in the branch of medical science that deals with the incidence and control of disease and injury

euthanasia mercy killing; the practice of killing terminally ill or injured persons in a relatively painless way either directly or allowing them to die by giving them incomplete treatment

growth hormone a hormone secreted by the pituitary gland that regulates growth; low levels of growth hormone may be linked to psychological disorders in persons who consider suicide

hara-kiri suicide by disembowelment practiced by Japanese warriors; carried out to protect honor or decreed by a court in lieu of a death penalty

hormones substances carried in the bloodstream that regulate many bodily processes by stimulating cell activity

hot line a telephone service through which volunteers offer anonymous callers sympathy, advice, and referrals on where to receive further help

insomnia the abnormal and drawn-out inability to get adequate amounts of sleep

kamikaze pilots members of a World War II Japanese air attack corps who made suicidal crashes on their targets

marijuana a psychoactive drug derived from the hemp plant

neonatal relating to an infant during the first month following birth

neurotransmitter a chemical released by neurons that transmits nerve impulses from one neuron to another

opiate a narcotic drug containing or derived from opium; induces sleep and alleviates pain

pituitary gland a small oval gland attached to the brain that secretes hormones relating to basic body functions, including growth and development, muscle contraction, and reproduction

psychoactive drugs drugs that chemically affect perception or behavior

risk factors in the case of suicide, the circumstances that predispose a person to consider or commit suicide; range from childhood difficulties to personal problems to chemical imbalances

sedative a drug or other agent that induces feelings of increased relaxation at first, leading eventually to sluggishness and lack of motor coordination

serotonin a neurotransmitter, an imbalance of which may be linked to some forms of depression

sociology the science that studies the structure, development, and behavior of groups of human beings

stimulant any drug or other agent that temporarily increases brain activity and produces the sensation of greater energy, euphoria, and increased alertness

suicide self-inflicted death

suicidologist one who studies suicide

suttee a custom in which a Hindu widow allows herself to be cremated on her husband's funeral pyre as a final display of love and respect

INDEX

PICTURE CREDITS

Laura Dolce received her B.A. in communications from Fordham University in 1986. She currently works as a writer and editor and lives in Middletown, New York, with her husband and daughter.

Solomon H. Snyder, M.D., is Distinguished Service Professor of Neuroscience, Pharmacology, and Psychiatry and director of the Department of Neuroscience at the Johns Hopkins University School of Medicine. He has served as president of the Society for Neuroscience and in 1978 received the Albert Lasker Award in Medical Research for his discovery of opiate receptors in the brain. Dr. Snyder is a member of the National Academy of Sciences and a Fellow of the American Academy of Arts and Sciences. He is the author of *Drugs and the Brain, Uses of Marijuana, Madness and the Brain, The Troubled Mind,* and *Biological Aspects of Mental Disorder.* He is also the general editor of Chelsea House's ENCYCLOPEDIA OF PSYCHOACTIVE DRUGS.

C. Everett Koop, M.D., Sc.D., is former Surgeon General, deputy assistant secretary for health, and director of the Office of International Health of the U.S. Public Health Service. A pediatric surgeon with an international reputation, he was previously surgeon-in-chief of Children's Hospital of Philadelphia and professor of pediatric surgery and pediatrics at the University of Pennsylvania. Dr. Koop is the author of more than 175 articles and books on the practice of medicine. He has served as surgery editor of the *Journal of Clinical Pediatrics* and editor-in-chief of the *Journal of Pediatric Surgery.* Dr. Koop has received nine honorary degrees and numerous other awards, including the Denis Brown Gold Medal of the British Association of Paediatric Surgeons, the William E. Ladd Gold Medal of the American Academy of Pediatrics, and the Copernicus Medal of the Surgical Society of Poland. He is a chevalier of the French Legion of Honor and a member of the Royal College of Surgeons, London.